HMH SCIENCE DIMENSIONS™

Grade 1

This Write-In Book belongs to

_____

Teacher/Room

_____

Houghton Mifflin Harcourt™

Consulting Authors

Michael A. DiSpezio
Global Educator
North Falmouth, Massachusetts

Marjorie Frank
Science Writer and Content-Area
  Reading Specialist
Brooklyn, New York

Michael R. Heithaus, PhD
Dean, College of Arts, Sciences & Education
Professor, Department of Biological Sciences
Florida International University
Miami, Florida

Cary Sneider, PhD
Associate Research Professor
Portland State University
Portland, Oregon

All images ©Houghton Mifflin Harcourt, Inc., unless otherwise noted

Front cover: ©HMH

Back cover: *chick hatching* ©wisawa222/Shutterstock

Program Advisors

Classroom Reviewers

You are a scientist.
You are naturally curious.

You may have wondered things such as these.

Why does ice melt?

Why does your heart beat?

Where does thunder come from?

What do animals need to grow?

HMH SCIENCE DIMENSIONS™

will **SPARK** your curiosity.

Where do you see yourself when you grow up?

Draw what you want to do when you grow up.

Be a scientist.
Work like real scientists work.

Solve problems.

Explain why.

Have fun.

Be an engineer.
Solve problems like engineers do.

Design.

Solve.

Test.

Explain your world.
Start by asking questions.

Do.

Think.

Share.

There is more than one way to the answer. What is yours?

Work in teams.

Make a claim.

Support with evidence.

Unit 3 • Light....................................79

Life Science
Unit 4 • Plant and Animal Structures 137

Unit 5 • Living Things and Their Young 217

Safety in Science

Doing science is fun. But a science lab can be dangerous. Know the safety rules and listen to your teacher.

- 🚫 Do not eat or drink anything.
- 🚫 Do not touch sharp things.
- ✔ Wash your hands.
- ✔ Wear goggles to keep your eyes safe.
- ✔ Be neat and clean up spills.
- ✔ Tell your teacher if something breaks.
- ✔ Show good behavior.

Circle the pictures where a safety rule is being followed. Place an X on the pictures where a safety rule is not being followed.

Unit 1
Engineering and Technology

Unit Project • Pocket Lock-It

How can you keep things from falling out of a jacket pocket? Investigate to find out.

Unit 1 At a Glance

Unit Vocabulary

engineer a person who uses math and science to solve everyday problems (p. 6)

problem something that needs to be fixed or made better (p. 6)

solution something that fixes a problem (p. 6)

technology what engineers make to meet needs and solve problems (p. 9)

design process a plan with steps used to find solutions to problems (p. 20)

Vocabulary Game • Guess the Word

Materials
- 1 set of word cards

How to Play
1. Work with a partner to make word cards.
2. Place the cards face down in a pile.
3. One player picks the top card but does not show it.
4. The second player asks questions until they guess the word correctly.
5. Then the second player takes a card.

People make things to solve problems.

By the End of This Lesson

I will be able to describe how people understand problems and make technology.

Understand the Problem

Mia uses headphones to listen to music.
She keeps them in her pocket.

Explore online. ▶

Can You Explain It?

✏️ What is Mia's problem? How can you
understand the problem to solve it?

_____

_____

_____

What Is an Engineer?

Explore online. ▶

Engineers use science and math to build bridges.

Engineers make cars that do not need gas.

Engineers build rides that are safe.

An **engineer** is a person who uses math and science to solve problems. A **problem** is something that needs to be fixed or made better. Engineers look for solutions. A **solution** is something that fixes a problem.

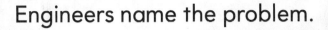

Explore online. ▶

Engineers name the problem.

Engineers ask questions about the problem. They observe and gather information.

Engineers can solve a problem. First they have to understand the problem.

What do engineers do? Choose all correct answers.

Ⓐ find and solve problems

Ⓑ use math and science

Ⓒ ask questions

✋ **Apply What You Know**

Evidence Notebook • Act like an engineer. Put headphones in your pocket. Walk around the room for two minutes. What problem happens? Work with a group. Ask questions about the problem. Write down your questions. Then make observations and gather evidence.

💡 **Asking Questions and Defining Problems**
Go to the online handbook for tips.

What Is Technology?

Explore online. ▶

Technology can help someone walk.

Technology can be simple, like a hammer.

Technology is what engineers make to meet needs and solve problems. Technology can even be an idea from nature. The idea for planes came from birds.

Which objects are technology? Choose all correct answers.

Ⓐ a lamp

Ⓑ a tree

Ⓒ a pencil

Do the Math! • This tally chart shows how children in one class use technology each day.

Classroom Technology	
pencil	卌
tablet	卌 ||||
cell phone	卌 |

Interpret Data Go to the online handbook for tips.

How many more children use a tablet than a cell phone each day?

_____ more children

Recall Information Go to the online handbook for tips.

Apply What You Know

Read, Write, Share! • **Evidence Notebook** • Find three kinds of technology. How do you know each one is technology? What problems do they solve? Use evidence to answer the questions. Write your answers in your Evidence Notebook.

Hands-On Activity

Engineer It • Solve the Problem

Materials • headphones • classroom materials

Ask a Question

_____

Test and Record Data   **Explore online.** ▶

Step 1

Explain the problem.
Gather information about
the problem.

Step 2

Plan two solutions to the problem.

Step 3

Use the classroom materials to build your solutions.

Step 4

Share your solutions. Talk about how the shape of each design solved the problem.

Make a claim that answers your question.

What is your evidence?

Take It Further

Careers in Science & Engineering •
Packaging Engineer

Explore more online.

Transportation Timeline

Explore online. ▶

What do packaging engineers do? Here's a hint. You see their work on store shelves every day.

They design boxes and other packages. They use computers to plan their ideas.

Then they test their ideas. They drop and crush the packages! They make sure what is inside is protected.

A factory builds the final packages.

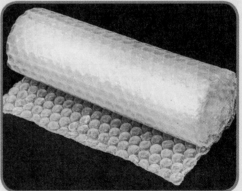

Draw a line to match each object with the best way to package it.

Lesson Check

Name_____

Explore online. ▶

Can You Explain It?

✏️▷ What is Mia's problem? How can you understand the problem to solve it?

Be sure to

• Name Mia's problem.

• Tell the steps needed to understand the problem to solve it.

_____

_____

_____

_____

Self Check

1. What does an engineer do first?

   (A) gather information about a problem

   (B) find a solution to a problem

   (C) name a problem

2. Which objects are examples of technology? Circle all correct answers.

3. Which is a problem technology could solve?

  Ⓐ Maya lost a letter in her house.

  Ⓑ Hector does not agree with his sister.

  Ⓒ Theo's backpack straps are hard to wear.

4. What does the picture show?

  Ⓐ an engineer

  Ⓑ technology

  Ⓒ a problem

5. How do engineers understand a problem? Choose all correct answers.

  Ⓐ They ask questions.

  Ⓑ They observe things.

  Ⓒ They gather information.

Engineers solve big and small problems.

By the End of This Lesson
I will be able to describe and use a design process to solve a problem.

The Pulling Dog Problem

Explore online.

Everyday problems need solutions.
Max's dog keeps pulling on its leash.

Can You Solve It?

How would you design a leash to solve
the problem of a dog pulling during a walk?

_____

_____

_____

© Houghton Mifflin Harcourt

Step 1–Define a Problem

Explore online.

A Design Process

1 Define a Problem

▼

2 Plan and Build

▼

3 Test and Improve

▼

4 Redesign

▼

5 Communicate

How can we solve problems? One way is to follow a design process. A **design process** is a plan with steps that helps engineers find good solutions.

The treats for Tara's dog keep crumbling when she puts them in her pocket. It's messy! This is a problem. She needs to find a way to protect the treats.

Tara defines her problem. She gathers information about the problem.

Explore online.

✏️ What is Step 1 of a design process?

_____

Apply What You Know

Define a problem in your classroom. Make observations and gather information about the problem. Talk with others about the problem. Tell what you know about it.

Asking Questions and Defining Problems
Go to the online handbook for tips.

Step 2–Plan and Build

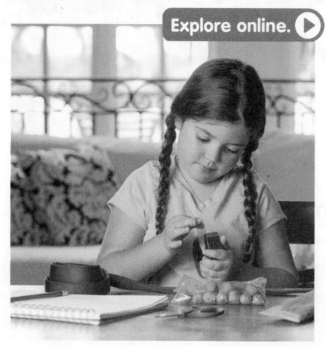

Explore online.

What does Tara do next? She thinks of an idea for two solutions that will hold and protect the treats. She chooses her materials and builds the solutions.

You want to plan a solution. What is the first thing you should do?

_____

Apply What You Know

Think about the classroom problem you found. Think of an idea for two solutions. Make models of your solutions. Then, choose materials and build your solutions. Follow your models.

Developing and Using Models • Structure and Function Go to the online handbook for tips.

© Houghton Mifflin Harcourt

Step 3–Test and Improve

Explore online. ▶

Tara tests her solutions. They both protect the treats. But the baggy is hard to use, and the long paper roll is tricky to tip over. Can she make either of her solutions better?

✏️➡ What do you do after you build your solutions?

Apply What You Know

Evidence Notebook • Test your solutions for solving the classroom problem. Which one works best? Use evidence to explain. How would you improve the solution?

Analyzing and Interpreting Data Go to the online handbook for tips.

Step 4–Redesign

Tara decides to redesign her paper towel roll solution. She thinks a short roll will work better, so she cuts it in half. Then she tests the solution again. It works!

Explore online.

What happens at Step 4 of a design process?

_____

_____

Apply What You Know

Evidence Notebook • Now redesign your solution for the classroom problem. Test the solution. Does the new solution work better? Use evidence to tell how you know.

Step 5–Communicate

Explore online. ▶

Tara draws her final solution and takes a picture of her drawing. You can draw, take photos, or write notes to tell about a solution. Why is this step important? People may want to use your idea. They may try to make it better.

How can you communicate the solution to a problem? Choose all correct answers.

Ⓐ Make drawings.

Ⓑ Take photos.

Ⓒ Write notes.

Do the Math! • Brooke builds two solutions to stop her cat from scratching a chair. She tests Solution 1 three times. She tests Solution 2 six times. Add tally marks to the chart to show how many times Tara tests Solution 2.

Represent Data Go to the online handbook for tips.

Number of Times Scratched	
Solution 1	III
Solution 2	

Apply What You Know

You found a solution to your classroom problem. Now tell others about it. Draw a picture of the solution. Write notes to tell what you did. Take some photographs.

Name_____

Hands-On Activity

Engineer It • Protect the Legs!

Materials • a fork • classroom materials
• a small chair

Ask a Question

_____

Test and Record Data Explore online. ▶

Step 1

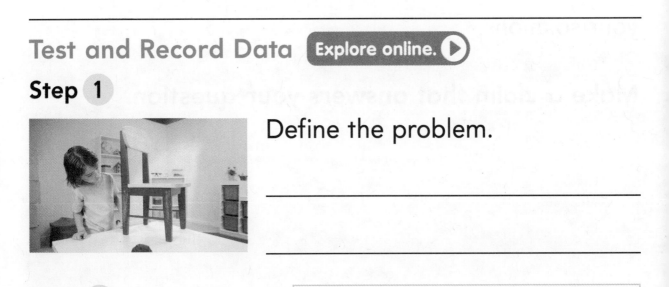

Define the problem.

_____

_____

Step 2

Plan two solutions.
Choose the materials
you will use.

Step 3

Build your solutions. Follow your plan.

Step 4

Test your solutions. Look for ways to improve your designs.

Step 5

Think of a way you could redesign your solutions. Share your solutions.

Make a claim that answers your question.

What is your evidence?

Take It Further

People in Science & Engineering •
Mary A. Delaney

Explore more online.

Solve a Paw-blem

Explore online. ▶

Did you know that a leash we use today was invented a long time ago?

New York City in 1908

Mary A. Delaney lived in New York City in 1908. She saw a problem with leashes people were using. They did not keep dogs close.

Delaney's leash today

Delaney made a leash that could pull out and back. Over time, people made the idea better.

© Houghton Mifflin Harcourt • Image Credits: (t) ©Everett Collection Historical/Alamy; (b) ©Lynne Carpenter/Getty Images

Take It Further

Read, Write, Share! • Go online. Research a dog leash design. How does it work? What problem does it solve? Make a report to share what you learned. You can use a computer or a tablet. Add pictures to show the leash design.

Write to Inform and Explain
Go to the online handbook for tips.

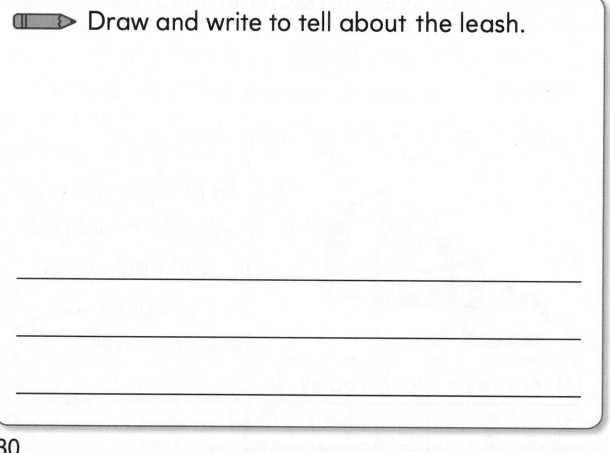

Draw and write to tell about the leash.

Lesson Check

Explore online. ▶

Can You Solve It?

✏️ How would you design a leash to solve the problem of a dog pulling during a walk? Be sure to

• Name the steps in a design process.

• Tell how you would use the steps to solve the problem.

_____

_____

_____

_____

Self Check

1. How do you understand a problem in Step 1 of a design process? Choose all correct answers.

   Ⓐ Ask questions.

   Ⓑ Make observations.

   Ⓒ Gather information.

2. Which step of a design process does this photo show?

   Ⓐ Define a Problem

   Ⓑ Plan and Build

   Ⓒ Communicate

3. Gabriel uses a design process to build a back scratcher. He tests the back scratcher. It is not long enough. What should he do next?

   Ⓐ Throw out the back scratcher.

   Ⓑ Communicate his solution.

   Ⓒ Find ways to improve it.

4. Kim builds a clay boat. The boat needs to be strong enough to hold a few pennies. How will Kim know her boat works?

Ⓐ She will test to find out if the boat floats.

Ⓑ She will test to find out if the pennies float.

Ⓒ She will test to find out if the water is high enough.

5. Juan builds a shelf for his books. The shelf keeps falling over. He finds new materials and rebuilds it. What problem is he solving?

Ⓐ Juan's books are not light enough.

Ⓑ Juan's shelf is not strong enough.

Ⓒ Juan does not have enough books.

Unit 1 Performance Task
Engineer It • Build a House

Materials

- cardboard
- tape
- other classroom materials
- paper
- scissors
- craft sticks
- fan or blow dryer

STEPS

Step 1

Define a Problem You want to build a house that can not be blown down by wind.

Step 2

Plan and Build Plan at least two solutions. Think about the materials you will need. Build your solutions.

Step 3

Test and Improve Test your solutions. How can you improve your solutions?

Step 4

Redesign Make changes to the materials or how you put the materials together. Test your new solutions.

Step 5

Communicate Share your solutions. Explain which materials you used and why you chose them. Use evidence to tell how your solutions solve the problem.

✔ Check

_____ I built two solutions.
_____ I tested my solutions.
_____ I redesigned my solutions.
_____ I shared my solutions with others.

Unit 1 Review

Name _____

1. What does an engineer do? Choose all correct answers.
   - Ⓐ uses math and science to solve problems
   - Ⓑ follows a design process
   - Ⓒ makes new technology

2. What is the last thing an engineer does to solve a problem?
   - Ⓐ gather information
   - Ⓑ define the problem
   - Ⓒ build a solution

3. Which objects in the picture are examples of technology? Choose all correct answers.
   - Ⓐ fishing pole
   - Ⓑ dock
   - Ⓒ lake

4. Kayla is learning to ride a bike. What technology solves the problem of her falling over?
   - Ⓐ a helmet
   - Ⓑ sneakers
   - Ⓒ training wheels

5. Which problem can Derek solve with technology?

Ⓐ Derek can not find a piece of paper.

Ⓑ Derek has a flat tire on his bike.

Ⓒ Derek can not make up his mind about what snack he wants.

6. Which technology can help solve each problem? Draw a line to match each problem to the technology that can help solve it.

7. Which is true about a problem?
   Ⓐ Problems only have one solution.
   Ⓑ Problems can have many solutions.
   Ⓒ Problems can only be solved by engineers.

8. Jacob finds a problem. He asks questions,
   makes observations, and gathers data.
   What should he do next?
   Ⓐ Plan and Build
   Ⓑ Test and Improve
   Ⓒ Redesign

9. What step of a design process
   does the picture show?
   Ⓐ Define a Problem
   Ⓑ Communicate
   Ⓒ Test and Improve

10. Which are ways to communicate a solution?
    Choose all correct answers.
    Ⓐ take photos or draw pictures
    Ⓑ write notes to tell about it
    Ⓒ ask questions and make observations

Unit 2
Sound

Unit Project • Explore Sound

How do vibrations make sound?
Investigate to find out.

Unit 2 At a Glance

Unit Vocabulary

sound a kind of energy you hear when something vibrates (p. 44)

vibrate to move quickly back and forth (p. 44)

volume how loud or soft a sound is (p. 46)

pitch how high or low a sound is (p. 47)

communicate to share information (p. 60)

Vocabulary Game • Make a Match

Materials
- 1 set of word cards
- 1 set of definition cards

How to Play
1. Work with a partner to make word and definition cards.
2. Place the cards face up on a table.
3. Pick a word card, read the word, and match it to a definition.
4. If you make a match, keep the cards and play again.
5. If not, your partner takes a turn.

What Is Sound?

Sound can make materials move.

By the End of This Lesson

I will be able to explain that materials that vibrate make sound, and that sound can make materials vibrate.

Sound Makes Objects Move

A speaker makes sound. Look at what happens when water is placed over the speaker.

Explore online. ▶

Can You Explain It?

✏️ Why does the water move?

Beacause sound vibrate

Make a Sound

Sounds are all around you, but what is sound? **Sound** is a kind of energy that you hear when something vibrates. To **vibrate** is to move quickly back and forth.

Explore online. ▶

A hammer in the piano hits a string.

The string vibrates, or moves. It makes a sound you can hear.

When does a piano string make sound?

Ⓐ when it travels

Ⓑ when it vibrates

Ⓒ when it listens

Apply What You Know

Work with a group. Hold a metal ruler down on a table. Let half of the ruler hang over the edge of the table. Pluck the part of the ruler sticking out. What do you hear? Do tests to make different sounds. What causes the sound to change?

Cause and Effect Go to the online handbook for tips.

Volume and Pitch

Explore online. ▶

A siren makes a loud sound.

A whisper is a soft sound.

What is the difference between a siren and a whisper? They have different volumes. One is loud and one is soft. **Volume** is how loud or soft a sound is.

low pitch

high pitch

Sounds can also be high or low. **Pitch** is how high or low a sound is. You can hear a high pitch and a low pitch on a piano. The keys on one side of a piano make low sounds. The keys on the other side of a piano make high sounds.

✏️ **Look at the pictures. Write loud or soft to tell about the sound each thing makes.**

loud

soft

loud

soft

✏️ **Write high or low to complete the sentence.**
The sound of thunder has a ___high___ pitch.

Do the Math! • Pitch is measured with hertz. Hertz is a measurement for sound. A tuba can play a note with a pitch of 32 hertz. A cello can play a note with a pitch of 65 hertz.

Compare the numbers. Write <, >, or =.

32  62

Compare Numbers Go to the online handbook for tips.

Apply What You Know

Read, Write, Share! • Explore pitch in your classroom. Find objects that make sounds with a high pitch. Find objects that make sounds with a low pitch. List the objects. Talk with others about your list.

Participate in Discussions Go to the online handbook for tips.

What Makes It Move?

Explore online. ▶

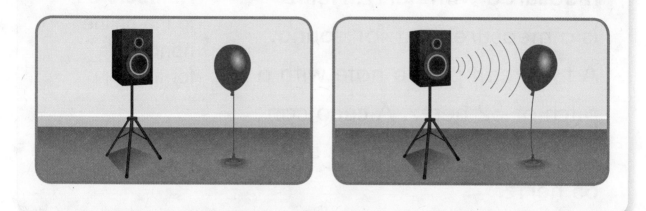

Look at the pictures. When the speaker is off, there is no sound. The balloon does not move. What happens when the speaker is on and sound begins to play? Sound waves from the speaker hit the balloon. The balloon moves.

Apply What You Know

Evidence Notebook • Work with a partner. Use a tuning fork and a glass of water to explore sound. Plan a test to show that sound can make materials vibrate. Use evidence to tell what happened.

Cause and Effect • Planning and Carrying Out Investigations Go to the online handbook for tips.

© Houghton Mifflin Harcourt

Hands-On Activity
Make Something Move with Sound

Materials

- a metal can
- cling wrap
- a rubber band
- rice
- a pot
- a wooden spoon

Ask a Question

_____

Test and Record Data [Explore online. ▶]

Step 1

Make a drum. Now put a handful of rice on top of the drum.

Step 2

Do the test. Bang a pot loudly very close to the drum.

Step 3

Record what you observe. Did the sound from the pot move the rice?

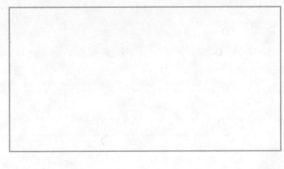

51

Step 4

Explain why the rice did or did not move.
Identify cause and effect.

Make a claim that answers your question.

What is your evidence?

Take It Further

People in Science & Engineering •
Ludwig van Beethoven

Explore more online.

Pitch In

Explore online. ▶

sheet music

Ludwig van Beethoven wrote music all of his life. He gave his first concert at age 7. He had a problem as he got older. He started to lose his hearing. Still, he found ways to write music. He felt the piano vibrate. He used sounds with low pitch because he could feel them better.

Beethoven wrote some of the most famous music in the world. Students study him. Orchestras play his music.

How did Beethoven keep writing music after he lost his hearing? Choose all correct answers.

Ⓐ He used low-pitch sounds.

Ⓑ He played music more loudly.

Ⓒ He felt his piano vibrate.

Lesson Check

Name _____

Explore online. ▶

Can You Explain It?

✏️ Why does the water move?

Be sure to

• Describe how sound can affect materials.

• Explain what causes the water to move.

_____

_____

_____

_____

Self Check

1. What causes sound?

   Ⓐ pitch

   Ⓑ energy when something vibrates

   Ⓒ volume

2. What is the main way the sounds of a siren and a whisper are different?

   Ⓐ They have different pitches.

   Ⓑ They are different kinds of energy.

   Ⓒ They have different volumes.

3. Which pictures show that sound is made when something vibrates? Circle all correct answers.

4. Can sound make materials move? Which test should you do to answer the question?

Ⓐ pluck a guitar string

Ⓑ bang a pot near a pile of rice

Ⓒ blow across the top of a water bottle

5. Tim does the test shown in this picture. What does this tuning fork test tell Tim?

Ⓐ Sound can make materials move.

Ⓑ Sounds can have high or low pitch.

Ⓒ Sounds can be loud or soft.

Engineer It • How Can We Communicate with Sound?

Music is one way to send messages with sound.

By the End of This Lesson

I will be able to explain how people use sound to send messages over a distance.

© Houghton Mifflin Harcourt • Image Credits: © Highwaystarz-Photography/iStock/

Sound Signals

Explore online. ▶

Dolphins use sound to send each other messages.

Can You Explain It?

✏️ How could you use sound to send a message over a distance?

use a whistle, ueasing a microphone.

Communicate with Sound

Explore online. ▶

How do people communicate with sound?
Communicate means to share information.

● Talking uses spoken words to share ideas.

● Music communicates feelings and ideas.

● Shouting is a way to communicate.

● Whistles send information.

© Houghton Mifflin Harcourt

What is a way to communicate with sound?
Choose all correct answers.

Ⓐ drawing

Ⓑ singing

Ⓒ talking

Apply What You Know

Work with a partner or small group. Take turns showing a way to communicate with sound. Name each way you communicate with sound.

whistle –

singing –

words –

shouting –

Communicate over Distances

Explore online. ▶

A megaphone makes a voice louder. People can hear the voice from farther away.

A cell phone sends out sound. It also receives sound from other cell phones.

Technology helps people communicate with sound over long distances.

Hands-On Activity

Engineer It • Communicate over Distance

Materials	• an object that makes noise
	• craft materials

Ask a Question

_____

Test and Record Data Explore online. ▶

Step 1

Go outside with your object. Have your partner walk 50 steps away.

Step 2

Make sound with your object. Try to communicate different things to your partner. Use different volumes and patterns with the sound.

Step 3

Plan and build something that makes your sound louder. Repeat Steps 1 and 2 to test your design.

Step 4

Record what you observed. Tell how you used sound to communicate over a distance. Tell how your design made your sound louder.

Make a claim that answers your question.

What is your evidence?

✏️ Which pictures show technology that helps people communicate with sound over distances? Circle the pictures.

Apply What You Know

Do the Math! • Work with a small group. Make a sound. How far away can another group hear it? Use your feet to measure the distance.

💡 **Use Nonstandard Units to Measure Length** Go to the online handbook for tips.

Send a Message

You use technology to communicate. How would your life be different without technology?

Influence of Engineering, Technology, and Science on Society and the Natural World Go to online handbook for tips.

Explore online.

You can use email to send messages. Without email, you might have to send letters. Letters take more time to send.

Dear Claudia SANCHEZ
Avenida de la Legua
22
Toledo 45005
ESPAÑA

You can take a cell phone anywhere. Before cell phones, people used different kinds of phones. People had to be in a place that had a phone.

What would life be like without email and cell phones?

Ⓐ Life would be the same.

Ⓑ People would have to use different technology.

Ⓒ There would be no technology at all.

Evidence Notebook • The clock in the next classroom is broken. You want to tell that class what time it is, but you can not leave your room. List ideas for solutions in your Evidence Notebook.

💡 **Designing Solutions** Go to the online handbook for tips.

✏️ Draw one of your solutions. Use evidence to tell why you think it will work.

_____

_____

_____

Take It Further
Careers in Science & Engineering •
Sound Engineer

Explore more online.

Morse Code

Explore online. ▶

Sound engineers study sound and how sound is made. They find ways to change sound to make it better.

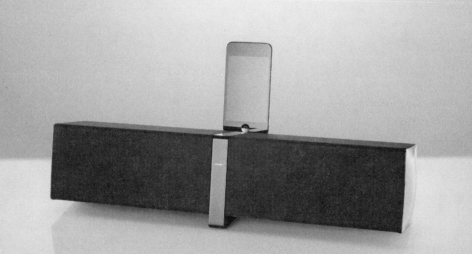

Sound engineers can work on small or big projects. They can make headphones or speakers, or they may do the sound for a big theater.

(b) © Gavin Roberts/Tap Magazine via Getty Images

Read, Write, Share! • Work with a group. Do research. Find another career where people use sound or study sound.

Participate in a Writing Project
Go to the online handbook for tips.

Draw or write about what you found.

theater

Lesson Check

Name _____

Explore online. ▶

Can You Explain It?

✏️ How could you use sound to send a message over a distance?

Be sure to

- Describe how people use technology to communicate.

- Explain how life would be different without this technology.

_____

_____

_____

© Houghton Mifflin Harcourt • Image Credits: ©ken kiefer 2/Cultura/Getty Images

Self Check

1. What do people do when they share information with others?

   Ⓐ They communicate.

   Ⓑ They measure.

   Ⓒ They vibrate.

2. John rings a bell to wake his sister in another room. What does this show?

   Ⓐ Life would be different without technology.

   Ⓑ Sound can be used to communicate over distances.

   Ⓒ People need many tools to communicate.

3. What did people do before they had cell phones? Choose all correct answers.

   Ⓐ They wrote letters.

   Ⓑ They used different kinds of phones.

   Ⓒ They did not communicate.

4. Which pictures show people using sound to communicate over distances? Circle the pictures.

5. If people no longer had email, what would they most likely do?

Ⓐ Give up on technology.

Ⓑ Stop communicating.

Ⓒ Write letters.

Unit 2 Performance Task
Communicate with Sound

Materials
- musical instruments

STEPS

Step 1
Does your school have a bell that rings at the start of the day? Make a list of the sounds your school uses to communicate messages. Talk about the list with others.

Step 2
Think of ways you can use sounds to communicate with another class. Plan what materials you will use.

Step 3
Decide what different sounds and patterns of sound will mean. Make a list to help people learn the sounds and their meanings.

Step 4

Test your sound signals. Can others understand your message?

Step 5

Compare your plan with the plans of your classmates. Talk about how they are alike and different.

✔ Check

_____ I talked about the sounds my school uses to communicate.

_____ I planned which materials I would use to communicate with sound.

_____ I made a list of what my different sounds mean.

_____ I tested my sound signals with others.

_____ I compared my plan to other plans.

Unit 2 Review

Name _____

1. **What happens when something vibrates?**
   Choose all correct answers.
   Ⓐ It moves back and forth quickly.
   Ⓑ It can make sound.
   Ⓒ It can make materials move.

2. **Beth thinks that materials that vibrate can make sound. Which test should she do to see this?**
   Ⓐ She should listen to sounds in her neighborhood.
   Ⓑ She should boil a pot of water.
   Ⓒ She should pluck a guitar string.

3. **Write loud or soft to tell the volume of the sound in each picture.**

_____

_____

4. Which sound has a high pitch?
   Ⓐ a growling dog
   Ⓑ a squeaky wheel
   Ⓒ a purring cat

5. Which pictures show how sound can move materials?

   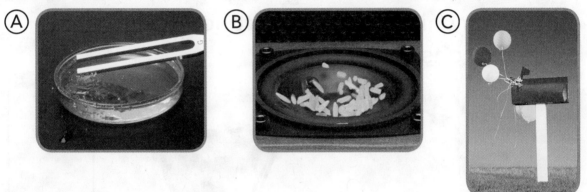

   Ⓐ   Ⓑ   Ⓒ

6. Gerard wants to do a test to show that sound can move materials. Which test should he do?
   Ⓐ place sand on a drum and bang a pot next to it
   Ⓑ pour a cup of sand into a large pot
   Ⓒ put sand in a shaker and shake it

7. What would happen if you plucked the string of the guitar in the picture? Choose all correct answers.
   Ⓐ It would vibrate.
   Ⓑ It would make a sound.
   Ⓒ It would make other materials in the room move.

8. What do people do when they communicate with sound?
   Ⓐ They vibrate.
   Ⓑ They write down data.
   Ⓒ They share information.

9. What kind of technology helps people use sound to communicate over a distance? Choose all correct answers.

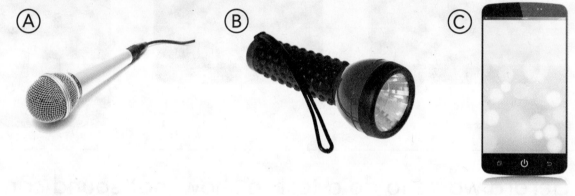

Ⓐ   Ⓑ   Ⓒ

10. Ava's dog runs across a field. She uses a whistle to call the dog back to her. What does this show?
    Ⓐ Ava needs many tools to communicate.
    Ⓑ Ava uses a sound to communicate over a distance.
    Ⓒ Ava could not call her dog without technology.

Unit 3
Light

Unit Project • Make a Rainbow

How can you make a rainbow? Investigate to find out.

Unit 3 At a Glance

Unit Vocabulary

light a kind of energy that lets you see (p. 84)

shadow a dark spot made when an object blocks light (p. 104)

reflect to bounce back from a surface (p. 118)

Vocabulary Game • Guess the Word

Materials
- 1 set of word cards

How to Play
1. Work with a partner to make word cards.
2. Place the cards face down in a pile.
3. One player picks the top card but does not show it.
4. The second player asks questions until they guess the word correctly.
5. Then the second player takes a card.

Light helps you see things.

By the End of This Lesson

I will be able to explain why you can see an object if it gives off its own light or if light shines on it.

Light in Darkness

It is nighttime. The sky is dark. But you can see fireworks in a dark sky.

Explore online.

Can You Explain It?

How can you see fireworks in a dark sky?

reflection of light

All About Light

Explore online.

The cave is dark. The lamp shines light inside it. This helps a cave explorer see the walls and objects.

Lights in a stadium help players see.

How can you see objects in dark places? You can see objects if light shines on them. Light from lamps helps people see. **Light** is energy that lets you see.

When can you see objects in dark places?

Ⓐ all the time

Ⓑ if you look carefully

Ⓒ when light shines on them

Do the Math! • Emma sees it get daylight. Her clock shows the time. What time does it get daylight?

Tell Time Go to the online handbook for tips.

Ⓐ 6:00

Ⓑ 12:00

Ⓒ 12:30

Explore online. ▶

bright light ▶ some light ▶ low light

The amount of light affects how much you can see. You can see a lot in a room with bright light. You see less when there is only some light. You see very little in low light.

✋ Apply What You Know

Read, Write, Share! • How can you see objects in a dark room? Think about the answer. Turn on a flashlight in a dark classroom. Make observations. Talk with your classmates. Add details to your answer.

Collaborate with Groups
Go to the online handbook for tips.

Hands-On Activity

Make Observations in Different Light

> **Materials** • drawing paper • a pencil

Ask a Question

_____

Test and Record Data [Explore online. ▶]

Step 1

Observe your classroom when there is a lot of light. How well can you see objects and details? Record your observations.

Things seem bright.

Not many shadows.

Step 2

Now observe the same room when it has only some light. How well can you see the same objects and details? Record your observations.

I can see darker and with difficulty.

Step 3

Finally, observe the room with very little light. What has changed? Record your observations.

The way I see changed. There was no light for me to see things

Step 4

Talk about your observations. What caused objects to look different?

Make a claim that answers your question.	**What is your evidence?**

I can see more in a lit room.

I could not see in a dark room.

See in the Dark

A campfire gives off its own light. You can see it in the dark.

A glow stick gives off its own light. You can see it in the dark.

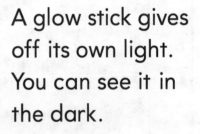

You can see an object in the dark if you shine light on it. You can also see an object in the dark if it gives off its own light.

Circle the object you could see best in a dark room.

You can not see much inside this dark cave. No objects inside give off their own light.

A spotlight lights up the cave. It shines on rocks and other objects. Then you can see them.

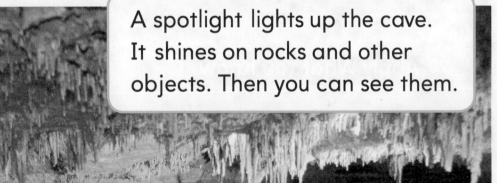

You can not see an object that does not give off light. You can not see an object that has no light shining on it.

A hiker can not see a rock in a dark cave.
Why not? Choose all correct answers.

Ⓐ The rock is darker than the cave.

Ⓑ There is no light shining on the rock.

Ⓒ The rock does not give off light.

Apply What You Know

Evidence Notebook • Work with a small group. Make your classroom dark. Think about this question—How can you see some objects in the dark? Together, design a simple test to answer the question. Make observations. Use evidence to answer the question.

Constructing Explanations and Designing Solutions • Cause and Effect Go to the online handbook for tips.

Take It Further
People in Science & Engineering •
Thomas Edison

Explore more online.

Animals That Glow

Explore online. ▶

Thomas Edison

Thomas Edison made many important inventions. One of his most important inventions was the light bulb. He made one of the first light bulbs in 1879. Light bulbs need electricity to work. Edison helped bring electricity to people's homes.

early lamp

(glass & wood)/Science Museum, London, UK/Bridgeman Images

Eastman House/Getty Images; (inset) @Early light bulbs: left: first commercial light bulb, right: electric filament lamp made by Thomas Alva Edison (1847–1931) in 1879

Edison also built switches and wires that made lights work.

How did Thomas Edison know that his light bulb worked?

(A) It was hooked up to wires.

(B) It needed power.

(C) It gave off light.

Lesson Check

Name ______________________

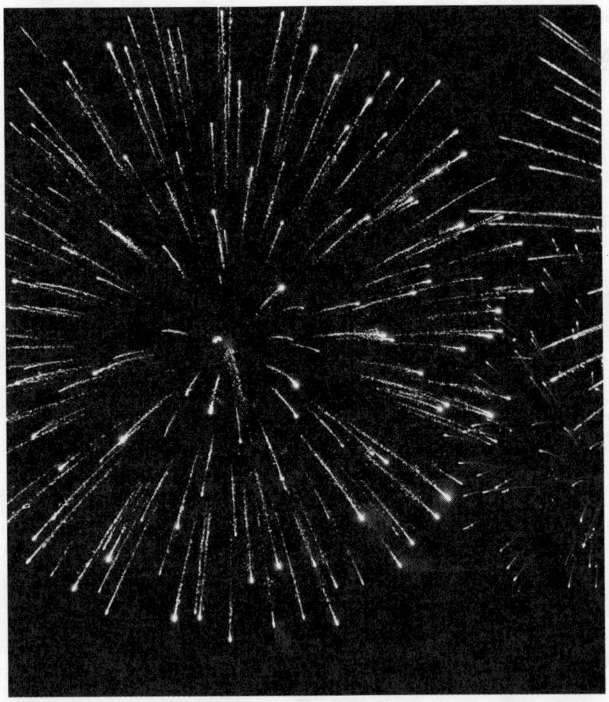

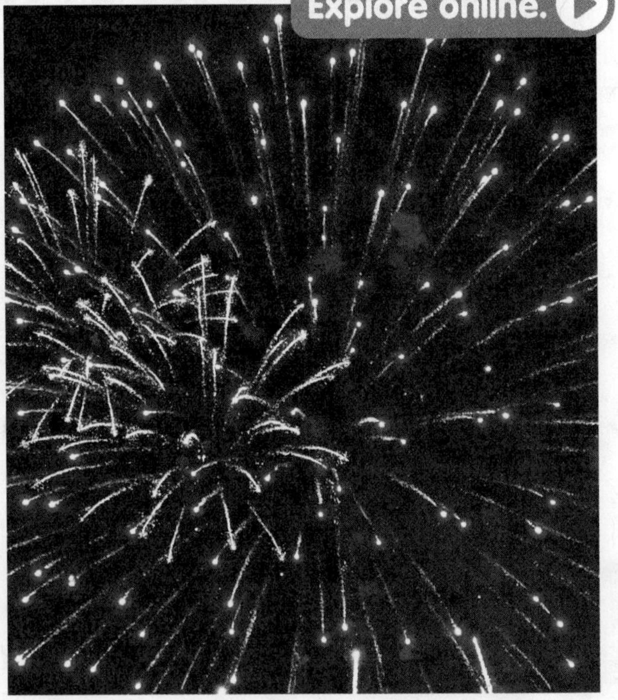

Explore online.

Can You Explain It?

How can you see fireworks in a dark sky?

Be sure to

- Explain when you can see objects in the dark.

____

____

____

____

Self Check

1. When can you see an object?
   Choose all correct answers.

   Ⓐ when it is dark

   Ⓑ when the object gives off light

   Ⓒ when light shines on the object

2. How could you test if an object
   gives off its own light?

   Ⓐ Put it under a lamp.

   Ⓑ Try to see it in the dark.

   Ⓒ Shine a flashlight on it.

3. Which objects give off their own light?
   Choose all correct answers.

   Ⓐ the sun

   Ⓑ glow sticks

   Ⓒ fires

4. You can see a few objects in this living room. Complete the sentence to tell why.

The living room is lit with _____.

Ⓐ many lamps

Ⓑ no lamps

Ⓒ one lamp

5. The campers see the fire. Why can they see it?

Ⓐ A light shines on the fire.

Ⓑ The space around the fire is dark.

Ⓒ The fire gives off its own light.

How Do Materials Block Light?

Materials block light in different ways.

By the End of This Lesson
I will be able to explain how shadows are made and that different amounts of light pass through materials.

Block the Light

This puppet show is in a dark room.
Even though it is dark, you can see
different shapes.

Explore online.

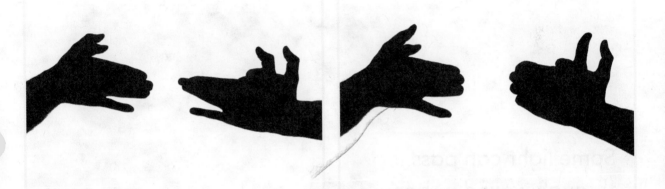

Can You Explain It?

How does the artist make the shapes?

Light hits the hand and
the light that is blocked by
the hand maeks a shadow.

How Much Light?

Explore online.

No light can pass through wood.

Some light can pass through waxed paper.

All light can pass through clear glass.

Different amounts of light can pass through different materials.

Hands-On Activity

Test How Light Passes Through Materials

Materials	• a flashlight	• clear plastic
	• frosted plastic	• plywood

Ask a Question

_____

Test and Record Data   Explore online. ▶

Step 1

Turn on the flashlight. Shine light through the clear plastic. Observe how much light passes through the plastic.

Step 2

Test the rest of the materials. How much light passes through each material? How do you know?

Step 3

Explain why different materials allow different amounts of light to pass through. Identify cause and effect.

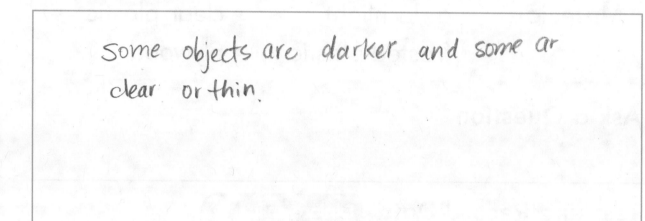

Some objects are darker and some ar clear or thin.

Make a claim that answers your question.

Does light pass through all things the same way?

What is your evidence?

The flashlight could not shine through the wood.

How much light passes through a clear glass bowl?

Ⓐ all light

Ⓑ some light

Ⓒ no light

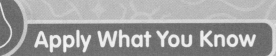

Apply What You Know

Do the Math! • Explore your classroom. Make lists of objects that let all light pass through, some light pass through, and no light pass through. Count and write how many objects are in each group.

Write Numbers
Go to the online handbook for tips.

All Light	Some Light	No Light
one.	froste door curtain	the fah and the wall and the roof.
window.	two.	three.

Shadows

Explore online.

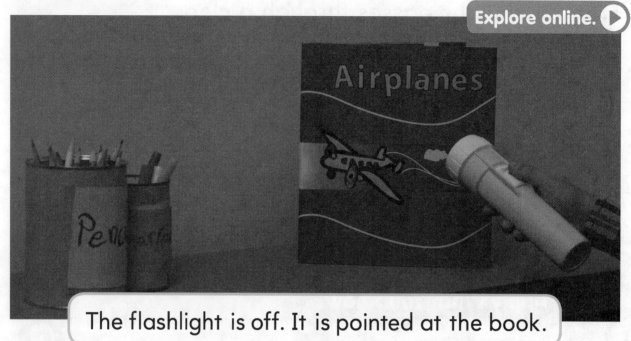

The flashlight is off. It is pointed at the book.

The flashlight is on. The book blocks the light and makes a shadow.

A **shadow** is a dark spot made when an object blocks light. The light does not pass through the object.

The size of a shadow changes when the light shining on the object moves.

What causes a shadow?

Ⓐ An object blocks light.

Ⓑ A dark spot behind an object blocks light.

Ⓒ Light shines on an object.

How will a book's shadow change if light moves closer to the book?

Ⓐ It will get smaller.

Ⓑ It will get bigger.

Ⓒ It will stay the same size.

Apply What You Know

Evidence Notebook • Work with a group. How does the shape of an object affect its shadow? Design a test using paper and light to answer the question. Do your test. Gather evidence. Use evidence to answer the question.

Planning and Carrying Out Investigations • **Cause and Effect** Go to the online handbook for tips.

Take It Further
Prisms

Explore more online.

Make a Sundial

Explore online. ▶

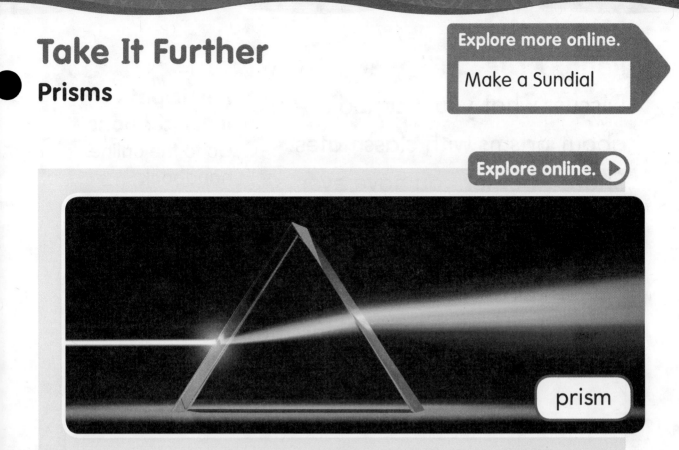

prism

A prism is a piece of glass. Light goes in one side of the glass. The light splits up. Colors come out the other side of the glass.

Raindrops can act like prisms. They can bend sunlight. This makes the colors of a rainbow.

Read, Write, Share! •

Discuss what you learned about prisms with classmates. Share whether you have ever seen a prism or a rainbow.

Participate in Discussions
Go to the online handbook for tips.

Draw or write to show what you talked about with your classmates.

_____

_____

_____

Lesson Check

Name _____

Explore online. ▶

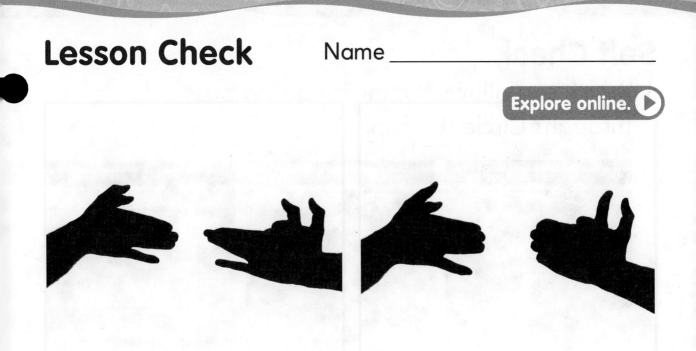

Can You Explain It?

✏▷ How does the artist make the shapes?

Be sure to

- Explain that different amounts of light can pass through different materials.
- Explain how shadows are made.

_____

_____

_____

_____

Self Check

1. Which cup allows the most light to pass through? Circle the cup.

2. How much light passes through each object? Match the object to the words that describe it.

No light passes through.	All light passes through.	Some light passes through.

3. Eli thinks that all objects block all light. How can he test his idea?

   Ⓐ He can make a shadow on a wall.

   Ⓑ He can move a light closer to an object.

   Ⓒ He can shine light on different objects.

4. Where is the shadow in this picture? Circle it to show your answer.

5. You make a shadow of your hand on a wall with a flashlight. You want the shadow to be smaller. How should you move the flashlight?

   Ⓐ Move it closer to your hand.

   Ⓑ Move it farther from your hand.

   Ⓒ Keep it in the same place.

Light can move from one place to another.

By the End of This Lesson

I will be able to explain how smooth surfaces reflect light and how to communicate with light.

Light in Your Eyes

Explore online. ▶

The sun's light shines right in Jayden's eyes.
Light in your eyes can be a problem.

Can You Solve It?

✏️▷ How could you point light away
from your eyes?

_____

_____

_____

Straight On

Explore online. ▶

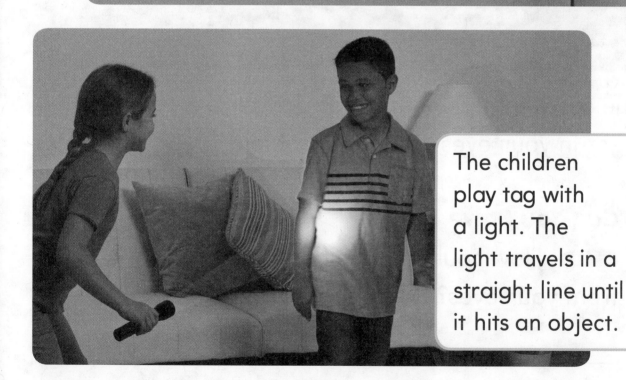

The light travels through the water in the tank. It travels in a straight line.

The children play tag with a light. The light travels in a straight line until it hits an object.

Light travels in a straight line until it hits an object.

When light hits an object, different things may happen. The light can pass through, be taken in, or bounce back.

Explore online.

The light hits the glass. All the light passes through the object.

The light hits the cardboard. Light is taken in by the cardboard.

The light hits the foil. The light bounces back.

What happens to light when it hits each object? Draw a line to match each picture to the correct label.

The light
passes through.

The light
is taken in.

The light
bounces back.

What does the light in the water tank show about light?

Ⓐ Light does not travel.

Ⓑ Light travels in a straight line.

Ⓒ Light never hits objects.

Apply What You Know

Evidence Notebook • Work with a group. Answer the question, How can we show that light travels in a straight line? Use cards and a flashlight. Use evidence to answer the question.

Cause and Effect Go to the online handbook for tips.

A New Direction

Explore online.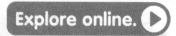

Look at the pictures to explore how surfaces can reflect light.

Light hits the mirror. It reflects off the mirror and moves in a new direction.

Smooth and shiny surfaces can reflect light. **Reflect** means to bounce back from a surface.

Explore online. ▶

When the mirror moves, the light moves in a different direction.

Light can move in a new direction when it hits a smooth, shiny surface.

✏️ Draw a surface that can reflect light.

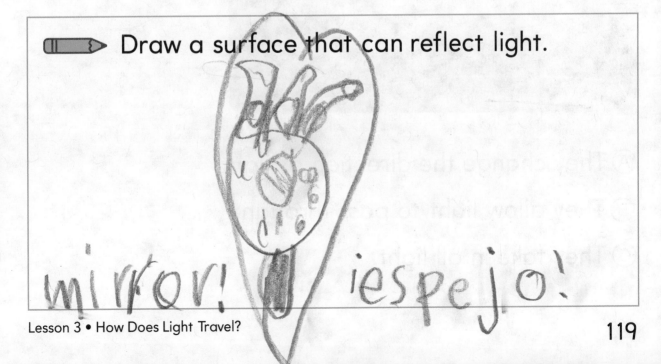

mirror! ¡espejo!

 Circle each object that reflects light.

What does this picture show about smooth, shiny materials?

Cause and Effect Go to the online handbook for tips.

Ⓐ They change the direction of light.

Ⓑ They allow light to pass through.

Ⓒ They take in all light.

Hands-On Activity
Test What Happens to Light

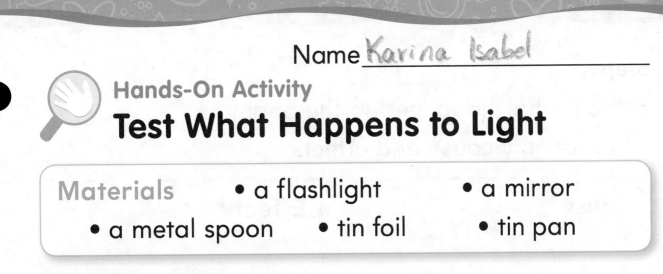

Materials	• a flashlight	• a mirror
• a metal spoon	• tin foil	• tin pan

Ask a Question

Test and Record Data   Explore online. ▶

Step 1

Plan a way to test how smooth, shiny surfaces affect a beam of light. Write your plan.

Step 2

Use the materials to do your test. Record what happens.

can - reflects light
spoon - on one side reflects
tin foil - reflects very little
tin pan - reflects some light
mirror - reflects the most

Step 3

Explain what happened to the beam of light. Identify cause and effect.

Cause		Effect
	▶	

Make a claim that answers your question.

How does light travels when it hits different materials?

What is your evidence?

Mirror reflects a lot of light

tin pan reflects less light

Do the Math! • A beam of light travels 5 feet. A mirror reflects it. The light travels 6 feet more. Then it bounces off a metal door and travels 2 feet more. How many feet does the light travel in all?

Ⓐ 11 feet

Ⓑ 13 feet

Ⓒ 15 feet

Solve Word Problems Go to the online handbook for tips.

✋ **Apply What You Know**

Evidence Notebook • Can you reflect light so it hits a spot you want? Work with a partner. Use a flashlight and three small mirrors to make light hit a spot you want. Then talk with your classmates. Collect evidence. Write and draw in your Evidence Notebook. Use evidence to explain if your test worked.

Planning and Carrying Out Investigations Go to the online handbook for tips.

© Houghton Mifflin Harcourt

Communicate with Light

Explore online. ▶

A traffic light communicates with colored lights. Green means go. Red says stop!

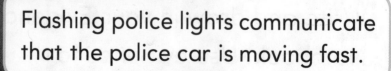

Flashing police lights communicate that the police car is moving fast.

© Houghton Mifflin Harcourt • Image Credits: (t) ©Keith Szafranski/Creatas Video/

The light from a lighthouse helps boats find their way. It also warns them of danger.

People can use light to communicate.
Different lights send different messages.

✏️ Circle the pictures that show ways to communicate with light.

🖐 **Apply What You Know**

Work with a partner or small group. Find a way to send a message with light. Make a plan. Gather materials. Test your plan. How will you know your message is understood? Redesign your plan. Make any needed changes, and test it again.

💡 **Planning and Carrying Out Investigations**
Go to the online handbook for tips.

Take It Further
Careers in Science & Engineering •
Camera Engineer

Explore more online.

Art with Light

Explore online. ▶

camera engineer

What do camera engineers do? They help design and build cameras for photos, movies, and videos. They may make large cameras for movies. They may make small cameras that go inside cell phones.

movie camera

cell phone camera

Read, Write, Share! •

What would you like to ask a camera engineer? Write at least two questions. Work with a partner to research answers to your questions. Write about what you found. Share what you learned with others.

Participate in a Writing Project • **Participate in Discussions**
Go to the online handbook for tips.

Lesson Check

Name _____

Explore online. ▶

Can You Solve It?

✏️▷ How could you point light away from your eyes?

Be sure to

- Explain what kind of surface can point light in a new direction.
- Describe how the surface points light in a new direction.

To point light away I could use a mirror or smooth shiny material to reflect the light somewhere else. When the light hits the mirror, it reflects off into a new direction depending on where I move the mirror.

Self Check

1. Ted thinks that smooth, shiny surfaces reflect light. How could he use a flashlight to test his idea?

    Ⓐ He could aim the light at a wood door.

    Ⓑ He could turn the flashlight on and off to send a message.

    Ⓒ He could observe what happens when light shines at a mirror.

2. How does light act when it hits each material? Draw a line to match each picture to the words that tell what happens when light hits it.

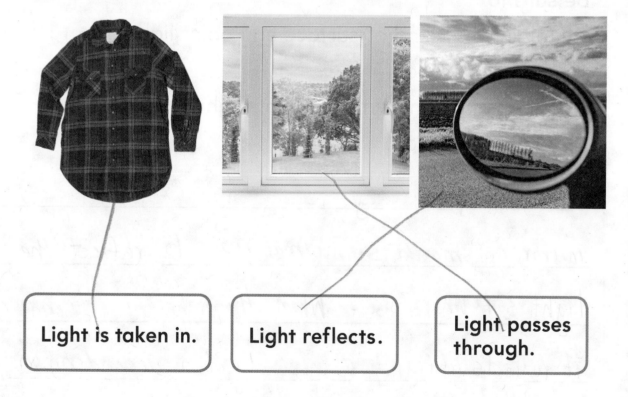

| Light is taken in. | Light reflects. | Light passes through. |

3. Anna builds a tool that uses light to communicate. How does Anna know if the tool works?

   Ⓐ Anna can send a message and find out if someone understands it.

   Ⓑ Anna can observe if light comes out of the tool.

   Ⓒ Anna can plan a message to send using her tool.

4. What happens to light when it hits a smooth, shiny piece of foil?

   Ⓐ It will be taken in.

   Ⓑ It will pass through.

   Ⓒ It will be reflected.

5. Which pictures show ways to communicate with light over distances? Circle the pictures.

Materials
- mirror
- masking tape
- paper

STEPS

Step 1

Attach the mirror to the wall. Look into the mirror. You see your reflection because light bounces off your face.

Step 2

Stand to the side and look in the mirror. What parts of the room do you see? Write or draw your observations.

Step 3

Work with a partner to cover the mirror. Think about where you each need to stand to see each other in the mirror. Mark those places with tape.

Step 4

Take the paper off the mirror.
Then stand on the tape. Can
you see your partner? If not, try
again. Write or draw to record
your observations.

Step 5

Compare your results with others.
Talk about how light traveled from
your face and bounced off the
mirror so your partner could see it.

✔ Check

_____ I observed my reflection in the mirror.

_____ I worked with a partner to guess where
to stand.

_____ I recorded my observations.

_____ I compared my results with others.

Unit 3 Review

Name _____

1. In which room could you see the most objects?
   Ⓐ a room with bright light
   Ⓑ a room with some light
   Ⓒ a room with low light

2. Why can you see fireworks in the night sky?
   Ⓐ The sky around the fireworks is dark.
   Ⓑ Fireworks give off their own light.
   Ⓒ Light shines on the fireworks.

3. What could you do to make the objects in this room easier to see?
   Ⓐ turn on more lamps
   Ⓑ turn off all lamps
   Ⓒ make the light lower

4. How much light can pass through each
   window? Match each window to the words
   that describe it.

| No light
passes through. | All light
passes through. | Some light
passes through. |

5. What causes a shadow?
   Ⓐ An object blocks light.
   Ⓑ An object gives off its own light.
   Ⓒ Light shines on an object.

6. You walk by a lamp and make a shadow on
   the wall. You want the shadow to be bigger.
   What should you do?
   Ⓐ Walk closer to the lamp.
   Ⓑ Step away from the lamp.
   Ⓒ Jump up and down in the same spot.

7. Which sentences are true about the way light travels? Choose all correct answers.
   Ⓐ Light can move around objects.
   Ⓑ Light travels in a straight line until it hits an object.
   Ⓒ Light can reflect off an object.

8. Which objects could you use to reflect light? Choose all correct answers.
   Ⓐ a piece of foil
   Ⓑ a wooden spoon
   Ⓒ a mirror

9. Brad tests what happens when he places a metal spoon in the path of a beam of light. What will he most likely see?
   Ⓐ The light will pass through the spoon.
   Ⓑ The spoon will take in all the light.
   Ⓒ The light will reflect off the spoon.

10. How do people use light to communicate over distances? Choose all correct answers.
    Ⓐ They use light to warn about danger.
    Ⓑ They use light to brighten a room.
    Ⓒ They use light to tell people to stop their cars.

Unit 4
Plant and Animal Structures

Unit Project • Research a Favorite Animal

How does your favorite animal meet its needs? Investigate to find out.

Unit 4 At a Glance

Unit Vocabulary

mimic to copy (p. 147)

gills body parts that take in oxygen from water (p. 183)

lungs body parts that take in oxygen from air (p. 183)

adaptation something that helps a living thing survive in its environment (p. 198)

environment all the living and nonliving things in a place (p. 198)

Vocabulary Game • Make a Match

Materials
- 1 set of word cards
- 1 set of definition cards

How to Play
1. Work with your partner to make word and definition cards.
2. Place the cards face up on the table.
3. Pick a word card, read the word, and match it to a definition.
4. If you make a match, keep the cards and play again.
5. If not, your partner takes a turn.

This tree has parts that help it live.

By the End of This Lesson
I will know the parts of a plant. I will be able to explain how observing plants can give people ideas to solve problems.

From Seed to Design

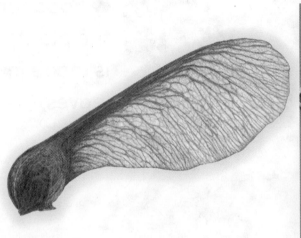

Explore online. ▶

Observing plants can give people ideas to solve problems.

Can You Solve It?

✏️ How did observing the maple seed give people ideas to make the helicopter blades?

_____

_____

_____

_____

Plant Parts

Explore online. ▶

A fruit holds seeds.

Food for the plant is made in leaves.

Water moves through the stem to other parts of the plant.

Seeds form in flowers. Seeds grow into new plants.

Roots take in water and hold the plant in the ground.

Thorns protect the plant from animals.

✎ Circle the part where seeds are made.

✎ Put an X on the part that holds the plant.

Each part of a plant helps the plant live.

142

Do the Math! • Observe a small plant with flowers. Count its parts. Show the data in the graph.

Represent Data
Go to the online handbook for tips.

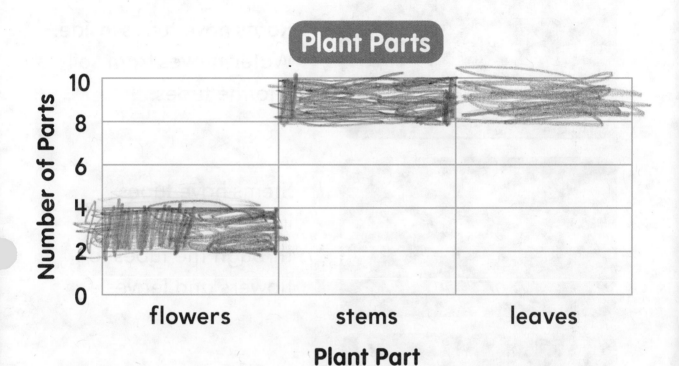

Plant Parts

Number of Parts

10

8

6

4

2

0

flowers   stems   leaves

Plant Part

Apply What You Know

Evidence Notebook • Observe a real plant. Draw and label it in your Evidence Notebook. Use evidence to describe what each plant part does.

Shape Up

How does the shape of each plant part help the plant live?

Explore online.

Structure and Function Go to the online handbook for tips.

Roots have tubes inside. Water moves from soil into the tubes.

Stems have tubes inside. Water moves through the tubes to flowers and leaves.

Thorns are sharp. Thorns keep animals from eating a plant.

Leaves have flat, green surfaces that catch sunlight. They also have openings that take in air.

Fruits are shaped to hold seeds inside. They protect seeds.

Look at the shape of this plant part. What does it do?

Ⓐ It moves water to the plant's parts.

Ⓑ It holds seeds inside.

Ⓒ It catches light.

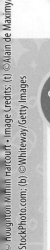

Apply What You Know

Evidence Notebook • Work with a group. Cover the leaf of a plant with dark paper. What do you think will happen to the leaf after two weeks? Use evidence to explain. Record your explanation in your Evidence Notebook.

Looking to Nature

Explore online.

Look at the pictures to see how observing plants can give people ideas.

Leaves take in sunlight to make food. The solar panels take in sunlight and change it into electricity.

146

Explore online. ▶

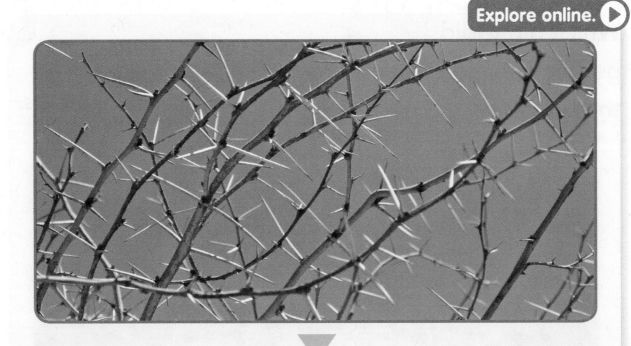

▼

Observing thorns gave people the
idea to make barbed wire fences.

People get ideas by observing plants.
People **mimic**, or copy, what they see in
nature to design things that solve problems.

Which plant did people copy to design the building?

Influence of Engineering, Technology, and Science
Go to the online handbook for tips.

Ⓐ   Ⓑ   Ⓒ

Apply What You Know

Read, Write, Share! • **Evidence Notebook** • Work with a partner. Research pictures of plants. Name solutions that look like those plants. Use evidence to tell how you know.

Participate in a Research Project
Go to the online handbook for tips.

Observe Plants

Explore online. ▶

This cactus has folds on its stem. The folds make shade for the plant. The shade keeps the cactus cool in the hot sun.

This tree can tilt its leaves. Then the sun does not hit the leaves directly. That keeps the tree cool.

This cactus shrinks down into the cool desert soil when the weather is hot.

Some plants have ways to keep cool in the heat.

Work with a small group. Observe a plant. Talk about its shape and what its parts do. Use ideas from oberving the plant to think of a new solution.

💡 **Constructing Explanations and Designing Solutions** Go to the online handbook for tips.

✏ Draw and label your solution. Write about how it solves a problem.

_____

_____

_____

Hands-On Activity

Engineer It • Observe Plants to Design

Materials • craft materials

Ask a Question

_____

Test and Record Data Explore online. ▶

Step 1

Explain the problem. Gather information about it.

Step 2

Think about the parts of plants. Plan your solution.

Step 3

Build your solution.

Step 4

Share your solution. Explain how observing plant parts gave you an idea for the solution.

Make a claim that answers your question.

_____

_____

_____

What is your evidence?

_____

_____

_____

Take It Further
People in Science & Engineering •
Janine Benyus

Explore more online.

Plants We Eat

Explore online. ▶

Janine Benyus helps people copy ideas from plants and animals to solve problems.

Benyus says she is a nature nerd!

She was named a "Hero of the Environment" for her work.

She has written six books about nature.

Ask Janine Benyus

Read, Write, Share!

Ask Questions Go to the online handbook for tips.

Work with a partner. Write questions for Janine Benyus. Then do an interview. One partner acts as Janine Benyus. The other partner asks questions. Then switch roles.

_____

_____

_____

Lesson Check

Name _____

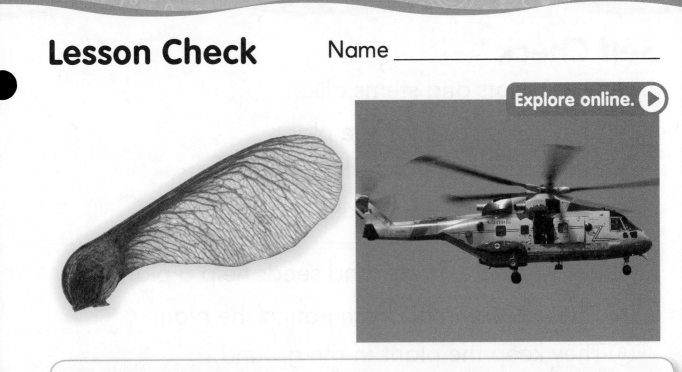

Explore online. ▶

Can You Solve It?

✏️ How did observing the maple seed give people ideas to make the helicopter blades?

Be sure to

• Tell how nature helps people solve problems.

_____

_____

_____

_____

_____

Self Check

1. How are roots and stems alike?

   Ⓐ They make food for the plant.

   Ⓑ They move water to other plant parts.

   Ⓒ They help the plant make new plants.

2. How do flowers, fruits, and seeds help a plant?

   Ⓐ They stop animals from eating the plant.

   Ⓑ They keep the plant in the ground.

   Ⓒ They help the plant make new plants.

3. Look at the seeds on the dog and the hook-and-loop fastener. How are they alike?

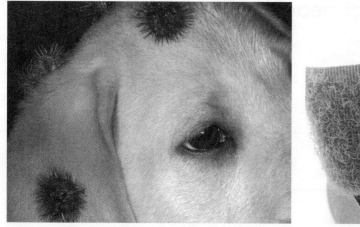 

   Ⓐ They stick to things.

   Ⓑ They take in sunlight.

   Ⓒ They are both found in nature.

4. Which plant did people observe that gave the idea for each solution? Draw lines to match the pictures.

5. Tari wants to design a way to take the salt out of seawater. Which plant would be best for her to study for ideas?

Ⓐ a tree that lives in salt water

Ⓑ a flower that lives in a garden

Ⓒ a cactus that lives in a desert

Engineer It • What Body Parts Help Animals Stay Safe?

Animals have body parts that keep them safe.

By the End of This Lesson

I will tell how body parts keep animals safe. I will be able to explain how observing animals can give people ideas to solve problems.

Staying Safe

A hedgehog rolls into a ball when it is in danger. It has spines all over. Animals do not want to eat a spiny hedgehog!

Explore online.

Can You Solve It?

✎➤ What ideas can you get from observing a hedgehog to keep something safe?

By rolling in a Ball

Moving Away from Danger

Explore online. ▶

A kangaroo hops on its back legs to stay safe. It uses its tail for balance.

A squirrel climbs to stay safe. It has sharp claws that help it climb.

A dolphin swims fast to stay safe. It uses its tail and flippers to swim.

A butterfly has wings to fly. This makes it hard to catch.

Some animals use body parts to move away from danger to stay safe.

Structure and Function
Go to the online handbook for tips.

✏️ Draw a line to match the animal to the way it moves in order to stay safe.

climbs   swims   flies

✋ **Apply What You Know**

Read, Write, Share! • **Evidence Notebook** • Work with a partner. Research how animals move to stay safe. Draw pictures of the animals. Write **runs, climbs, swims,** or **flies** to tell how they move. Use evidence to tell how you know.

💡 **Participate in a Research Project** Go to the online handbook for tips.

Hiding from Danger

Explore online. ▶

Explore how some animals have parts that help them hide from danger.

arctic hare

leaf insect

chameleon

These animals are hard to see in their environments. This helps them stay safe.

✏️➤ Circle each animal whose color could help it hide in this forest.

(toad) (squirrel) toucan

🖐️ **Apply What You Know**

What could you wear during a game of hide-and-seek to help you hide? Use an idea you got from observing an animal. Design something to wear. Share your idea.

Facing Danger

Explore online. ▶

A turtle has a hard shell that keeps its body safe.

A porcupine has sharp quills that keep its body safe.

An eagle has sharp talons it uses to protect itself.

✏️ Draw a line under the name of the body part that keeps each animal safe.

Some animals have body parts that help them stay safe.

Apply What You Know

Evidence Notebook • Design a box to keep things safe. Use ideas from observing animals. Add parts to your box. Use evidence to explain how the parts keep it safe.

Structure and Function Go to the online handbook for tips.

Staying Safe in Weather

Explore online. ▶

A red fox has a thick coat of fur in winter. It keeps the fox warm.

A walrus has a thick layer of blubber, or fat. It keeps the walrus warm.

A jackrabbit has big ears. They give off heat to keep the jackrabbit cool.

A blue jay fluffs up its feathers to stay warm.

Animals have body parts that help them stay safe from the weather.

©GizmoPhoto/Getty Images; (tc) ©Christopher Wood/Shutterstock; (b) ©Johann Schumacher/Getty Images

✎ Circle the body part that keeps the fox cool.

Evidence Notebook • Put one hand in an empty bag. Put the other hand in a bag with shortening. Put your hands into cold water. Tell which hand stays warmer. How does blubber keep animals warm? Use evidence to tell how you know.

Observe Animals

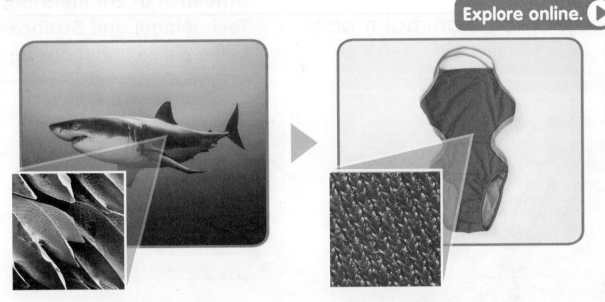

Engineers observed shark scales. They got an idea to make a kind of swimsuit fabric.

The feet of a gecko stick to things. Engineers observed gecko feet. They got an idea to make a tape that does not slip.

Engineers can get ideas by observing animals.

Lesson 2 • Engineer It • What Body Parts Help Animals Stay Safe?

167

Draw a line from each object to its animal model.

Influence of Engineering, Technology, and Science Go to the online handbook for tips.

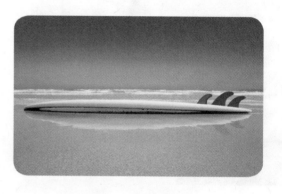

Apply What You Know

Do the Math! • Design a paper airplane. Look at pictures of birds for ideas. Build and test your airplane. Measure how far it flies. Build a new model. Measure how far it flies. Compare your results.

Use Nonstandard Units to Measure Length Go to the online handbook for tips.

Name_____

Hands-On Activity
Engineer It • Design a Shoe

Materials • ice • scissors • craft materials

Ask a Question

How can you protect your feet fom ice?

Test and Record Data Explore online. ▶

Step 1

Find a problem. How could you observe animals to get ideas to solve the problem?

fox, Polar bear, penguin bears f

Step 2

Plan two solutions.

Step 3

Build your solutions. Follow your plan.

Step 4

Test your solutions. How can you improve them?
Share your solutions with others.

_____

_____

_____

Make a claim that answers your question.

_____

_____

_____

What is your evidence?

_____

_____

_____

Take It Further

Careers in Science & Engineering •
Bioengineer

Explore more online.

New Body Parts for Animals

A bioengineer is a kind of engineer. Bioengineers design things to help people. They also look for ways to help the environment.

Explore online.

Bioengineers can work in labs. They make new medicines to help people who are sick.

Lesson 2 • Engineer It • What Body Parts Help Animals Stay Safe?

171

AFP/Getty Images; (t) ©Thomas Barwick/Stone/Getty Images

Bioengineers find new ways to clean air and water. They also help farmers grow food in ways that are safer.

What does a bioengineer do? Choose all correct answers.

Ⓐ helps clean air and water

Ⓑ studies rocks

Ⓒ makes new medicine

Lesson Check

Name _____

Explore online. ▶

Can You Solve It?

✏️ What ideas can you get from observing a hedgehog to keep something safe?

Be sure to

- Tell how a hedgehog's body parts keep it safe.
- Describe how observing the hedgehog gave you an idea.

_____

_____

_____

_____

Lesson 2 • Engineer It • What Body Parts Help Animals Stay Safe?

173

Self Check

1. Which body parts keep animals warm? Choose all correct answers.

   Ⓐ feathers

   Ⓑ blubber

   Ⓒ talons

2. What body part keeps a turtle safe from other animals?

   Ⓐ legs

   Ⓑ shell

   Ⓒ fur

3. Which animals would you use as models for making something that helps you swim faster? Circle the animals.

4. Which animal was used as a model for each object? Match the object to the animal.

5. Which material would you use to act like blubber? Choose the best answer.

Ⓐ rubber

Ⓑ wood

Ⓒ plastic

Animals have body parts that help them get food.

By the End of This Lesson
I will be able to tell how body parts help animals meet their needs. I will be able to explain how observing animals can give people ideas to solve problems.

Meeting Their Needs

A giraffe has a long neck and a long sticky tongue. It uses both to help it reach leaves.

Explore online.

Can You Solve It?

How can you get an idea from observing the giraffe to make a tool that reaches high places?

from somthing long

Lesson 3 • Engineer It • What Body Parts Help Animals Meet Their Needs?

177

Parts to Find Food

How do animals use eyes and ears to find food and stay safe?

Explore online. ▶

A tiger hunts mostly at night. It has eyes that can see in the dark!

A dragonfly has eyes that can see in all directions! This helps it find insects and stay safe from birds.

Draw a line under two ways animals use their eyes to find food.

A fox hunts for food. It has ears that face forward to hear animals.

A rabbit uses its nose to find plants. It has ears that turn. It listens for animals that might want to eat it.

A bat uses its ears to find food. The bat makes sounds. It listens for the sounds to come back to it.

Circle animals that eat other animals.
Draw a square around animals that eat plants.

Apply What You Know

Evidence Notebook • Compare your ears to animal ears. How can you get an idea from observing animal ears to make something that helps you hear better? Use evidence to explain. Write your answer.

Structure and Function
Go to the online handbook for tips.

© Houghton Mifflin Harcourt • Image Credits: (tl) ©Robert McGouey/All Canada

Parts to Eat Food

Explore online. ▶

A bear has sharp claws to grab fish. It has sharp teeth for tearing food.

A deer has front teeth for pulling up plants. It has flat teeth for chewing plants.

A frog has a sticky tongue to grab insects. It pulls the insect into its mouth to eat.

Animals use body parts to grab and eat food.

Lesson 3 • Engineer It • What Body Parts Help Animals Meet Their Needs?

Which body parts can animals use to grab food? Choose all the correct answers.

Ⓐ claws

Ⓑ teeth

Ⓒ tongue

Apply What You Know

**Do the Math! • Work with your class. Learn about human teeth. Find out how many flat teeth people have. Find out how many sharp teeth people have. Make a tally chart. Ask and answer questions about the data in the chart.

Organize, Represent, and Interpret Data
Go to the online handbook for tips.

Parts to Breathe and Take in Water

Explore online. ▶

A fish has gills. **Gills** are body parts that take in oxygen from water. Many animals that live in water have gills.

A zebra has lungs. **Lungs** are body parts that take in oxygen from air. Most land animals have lungs.

Animals need to take in oxygen. They have different body parts to help them take in oxygen.

An elephant uses its trunk to take in water. Then it moves the water into its mouth.

A fish lives in water. Its body needs water, too. A fish takes in water through its skin and gills.

A horse uses its mouth to drink water. It drinks like you do when you drink from a water fountain.

Animals need water to live. They have different body parts to take in water.

Structure and Function Go to the online handbook for tips.

✏️ Write **lungs** or **gills** to tell what each animal uses to take in oxygen.

_____ _____ _____

🖐 **Apply What You Know**

Read, Write, Share! • Look in books with a partner. Find one animal that uses lungs and one animal that uses gills. Use evidence to tell how you know.

Participate in a Research Project Go to the online handbook for tips.

Lesson 3 • Engineer It • What Body Parts Help Animals Meet Their Needs?

Animals as Models

Explore online. ▶

Look at the pictures. How did engineers get ideas from observing animals to solve problems?

Japan had a fast train with a problem. It made a loud sound going through tunnels. An engineer saw a bird that could dive without making a sound. He gave the train a pointy front like the bird's beak. Now the train goes through tunnels without making noise.

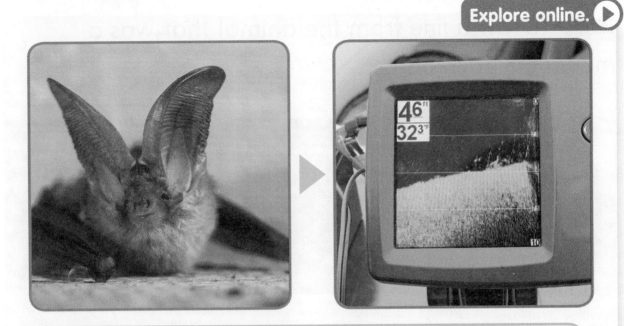

Engineers made a machine that sends sounds into water. The sounds bounce off fish to help fishing boats find them. Engineers got ideas from observing the sounds bats make.

Engineers got ideas from observing spider webs to build large nets. The nets collect drops of water from the air. The drops go into pipes.

Lesson 3 • Engineer It • What Body Parts Help Animals Meet Their Needs?

✏️➡️ Draw a line from the animal that was a model for each object.

  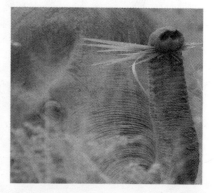

✋ **Apply What You Know**

Evidence Notebook • Look at classroom tools. What animal could have been a model for each tool? Discuss your ideas with classmates. Write your answers. Use evidence to tell how the animal could have been a model for the tool.

Hands-On Activity
Engineer It • Observe Animals to Design

> **Materials**   • animal books   • craft materials

Ask a Question

_____

Test and Record Data   Explore online. ▶

Step 1

Look in animal books. Observe how animals use their body parts to pick up food.

Step 2

Plan and build two solutions for picking up food.

```



```

Test your tool. Compare it with the tools of other classmates. How did observing animals give you an idea to solve the problem?

Make a claim that answers your question.

_____

_____

_____

_____

What is your evidence?

_____

_____

_____

Take It Further
Animals Can Use Tools

Explore more online.

Hear Like a Bat

Explore online. ▶

People use tools to help solve problems. What tools can animals use?

Dolphins use an ocean sponge to brush away sand to look for food. The sponge protects the dolphin's nose from rocks.

A sea otter floats with a rock on its chest. It hits a clam shell with the rock to crack it open. Then it eats the clam inside.

An elephant uses a tree branch to scratch its itchy back.

Lesson 3 • Engineer It • What Body Parts Help Animals Meet Their Needs?

191

Chimpanzees will sometimes go in the water. But chimps are not good swimmers.

© Houghton Mifflin Harcourt • Image Credits: ©Ronald Wittek/Image Bank/Getty

How do you think this chimp is using a stick to help it cross the river? Choose the best answer.

Ⓐ to help it swim

Ⓑ to help it paddle

Ⓒ to see how deep the water is

Lesson Check

Name _____

Explore online. ▶

Can You Solve It?

✏️▷ How can you get an idea from observing the giraffe to make a tool that reaches high places? Be sure to

- Tell how the giraffe uses its body parts to reach food in high places.

- Tell how observing the giraffe gives you an idea for making a tool that can grab something in a high place.

_____

_____

_____

Lesson 3 • Engineer It • What Body Parts Help Animals Meet Their Needs?

Self Check

1. Which body parts can animals use to find food? Choose all the correct answers.

   Ⓐ eyes

   Ⓑ ears

   Ⓒ gills

2. You want to design a sticky tool to grab objects. Which animal part would you use as a model?

   Ⓐ a groundhog's claws

   Ⓑ a bear's teeth

   Ⓒ a frog's tongue

3. Which of these animals would you use as a model for making a digging tool? Circle the correct answer.

4. Which body part do most land animals use to take in oxygen?

Ⓐ gills

Ⓑ lungs

Ⓒ ears

5. An engineer came up with an idea for a new kind of thumbtack. The pointy part of the thumbtack only comes out when it is being used. Which part of a cat do you think the engineer observed to get the idea?

Ⓐ cat claws that come out when a cat stretches

Ⓑ cat eyes that can see in low light

Ⓒ a cat tongue that can take dirt off fur

How Do Plants and Animals Respond to Their Environment?

Some animals move to get what they need.

By the End of This Lesson
I will be able to tell how plants and animals respond to the places where they live.

Plants Change to Grow

Have you ever seen trees like this? These trees are growing in unusual ways!

Explore online. ▶

Can You Explain It?

✏️➤ Why are the trees growing in unusual ways?

Because It's their
environment

Plant Places

Explore online. ▶

A rain forest has tall trees. Some plants grow on trees to reach the sunlight.

A desert gets very little rain. Many desert plants have thick stems and leaves to hold water.

Plants have adaptations to live in different places. An **adaptation** is something that helps a living thing survive in its environment. An **environment** is all the living and nonliving things in a place.

Apply What You Know

Do the Math! • Find a plant. Use connecting cubes to measure the height of its stem. Tell how its height might help the plant live in its environment.

Use Nonstandard Units to Measure Length
Go to the online handbook for tips.

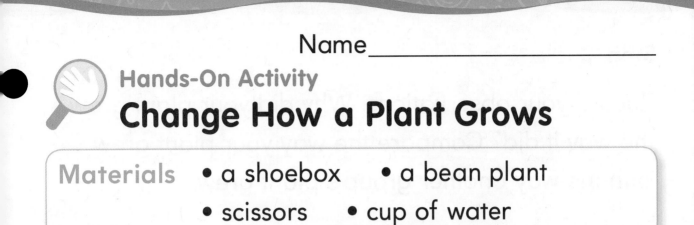

Hands-On Activity
Change How a Plant Grows

Materials	• a shoebox	• a bean plant
	• scissors	• cup of water

Ask a Question

_____

Test and Record Data Explore online. ▶

Step 1

Put the shoebox near a window. Place the plant in the box. Then close the box.

Step 2

Observe the plant for two weeks. Water the soil when it is dry.

Lesson 4 • How Do Plants and Animals Respond to Their Environment?

199

Step 3

Record your observations. Why did your plant grow the way it did? Compare the way your plant grew with the way another group's plant grew.

_____

_____

_____

Make a claim that answers your question.

_____

_____

_____

What is your evidence?

_____

_____

_____

Plants and Seasons

Explore online. ▶

How do plants survive in different seasons?

winter   spring   summer   fall

Some trees lose their leaves in winter because there is less sunlight. In spring and summer, more sunlight and water help new leaves grow. In fall, leaves change color and begin to drop off.

✏️ Underline what causes some trees to lose leaves in winter.

Apply What You Know

Evidence Notebook • What might happen if a plant did not get sunlight? Use evidence to explain your ideas. Draw and write about a way to test your ideas.

Cause and Effect
Go to the online handbook for tips.

Animals Use Senses

Explore online. ▶

A prairie dog uses its eyes and nose to notice the things around it. It will warn others if it sees or smells danger.

A great white shark has eyes that see well. It uses its ears to feel movements in the water.

A mouse does not see well at night. It uses its nose to smell for food. It uses its whiskers to feel in the dark.

Moles do not see well. What body parts do you think it uses to notice things and find food? Choose all the correct answers.

(A) nose

(B) eyes

(C) whiskers

![Apply What You Know]

Evidence Notebook • Work in a group. Talk about how you use your eyes, ears, nose, and hands to notice things around you. Use evidence to tell how you know. Share ideas.

Lesson 4 • How Do Plants and Animals Respond to Their Environment?

203

Animals on the Move

Explore online.

Why do some animals move to other places when the weather changes?

Every year, wildebeests travel a long way to find food. They move to where it rains and plants grow.

Gray whales live in cold waters. Every winter, they swim to warmer waters to have young.

In winter, emperor penguins move away from the ocean to have young. By summer, their young are big enough to swim and hunt.

Why do some animals move to another place when there are changes in the weather? Choose all the correct answers.

Ⓐ to find food

Ⓑ to hide from danger

Ⓒ to have young

Apply What You Know

Read, Write, Share! • Work with a partner. Learn about an animal in your area that moves when the weather changes. Draw a picture of the animal. Tell about why the animal moves. Use evidence to tell how you know.

Participate in a Research Project
Go to the online handbook for tips.

Lesson 4 • How Do Plants and Animals Respond to Their Environment?

205

Animals and Seasons

Explore online. ▶

What adaptations help animals live in the same place all year?

To get ready for winter, a groundhog eats a lot of food. Then it digs a home under the ground and sleeps all winter long.

A red fox grows thick fur and eats more to get ready for winter.

✏️▶ Draw a line under the words that tell how a groundhog gets ready for winter.

🖐️ **Apply What You Know**

Evidence Notebook • Learn about an animal in your area. How does it change with the seasons? Use evidence to tell how you know.

Take It Further

Careers in Science & Engineering •
Forest Ranger

Explore more online.

Insects in Winter

A forest ranger works to protect places where plants and animals live.

Explore online. ▶

A forest ranger watches for forest fires. A fire can quickly destroy plants and animals. It can also harm people visiting the forest.

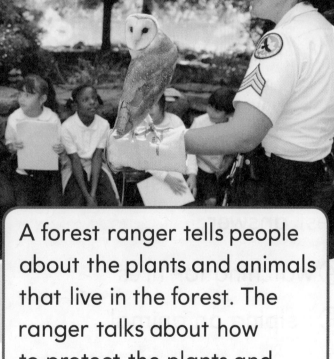

A forest ranger tells people about the plants and animals that live in the forest. The ranger talks about how to protect the plants and animals that live in a forest.

© Houghton Mifflin Harcourt • Image Credits: (l) ©Antonio Arcos/fotonstudio photography/Moment Open/Getty Images; (r) ©Stan Honda/Getty Images

Look at the photo of the forest ranger.

What is this forest ranger doing? Choose the best answer.

Ⓐ watching for fires

Ⓑ helping an animal

Ⓒ teaching people

Lesson Check

Explore online.

Can You Explain It?

Why are the trees growing in unusual ways?

Be sure to

• Tell what plants need to grow and live.

• Tell how these trees are growing to get the things they need in their environment.

_____

_____

_____

_____

Lesson 4 • How Do Plants and Animals Respond to Their Environment?

209

Self Check

1. Why do some plants grow on trees?

   Ⓐ to get water

   Ⓑ to take in air

   Ⓒ to get sunlight

2. What do trees get in the spring that causes them to grow new leaves?

   Ⓐ water and wind

   Ⓑ water and sunlight

   Ⓒ water and snow

3. How do animals use their eyes, ears, and nose to notice the things in their environment? Choose all correct answers.

   Ⓐ to sense danger

   Ⓑ to find food

   Ⓒ to eat food

4. Hector thinks that a plant will grow toward light. Which test should he do to prove that a plant grows toward light?

Ⓐ He should grow a plant in a box with no light.

Ⓑ He should grow a plant in a box that lets some light in.

Ⓒ He should grow a plant in a box with no water.

5. How does each animal get ready for winter? Match the animal to the words that describe how it gets ready for winter.

| grows thick fur | digs a home under the ground |

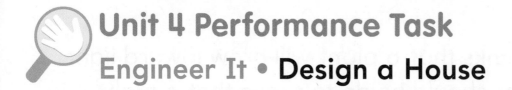
Materials
- books about water plants
- craft materials
- container of water

STEPS

Step 1

Define a Problem You want to design a house that could be built near or on the water.

Step 2

Plan and Build Look at plants that grow in or near the water. Use ideas from the plants to plan at least two solutions. Build your solutions.

Step 3

Test and Improve Test your solutions. How can you improve your solutions?

Step 4

Redesign
Make changes to the materials or how you put the materials together. Test your new solutions.

Step 5

Communicate Share your solutions. Compare solutions with others. Use evidence to tell how your solution solves the problem.

✔ Check

_____ I used ideas from plants to plan and build my house.

_____ I tested my house by putting it in water.

_____ I redesigned my house to make it work better.

_____ I shared my house with others.

Name _____

1. Look at the plant parts. How do they help the plant? Match the parts to the words.

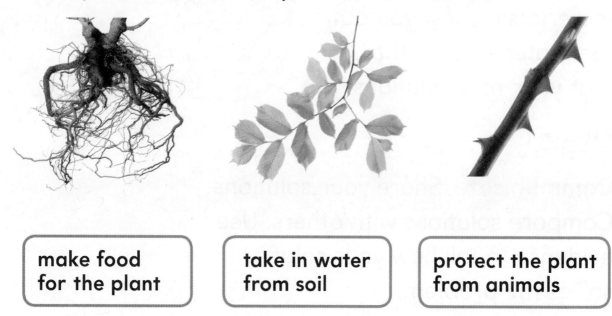

| make food for the plant | take in water from soil | protect the plant from animals |

2. Alonso wants to design a waterproof box that can float. Which plant would be best to study for ideas?

   Ⓐ a plant with seeds that are carried by wind

   Ⓑ a plant with seeds that are carried by water

   Ⓒ a plant with seeds that stick to the fur of animals

3. Which body part helps an eagle stay safe from other animals?

   Ⓐ horns

   Ⓑ shell

   Ⓒ talons

4. Look at the picture. Which body parts help keep this musk ox safe? Choose all correct answers.

Ⓐ thick fur

Ⓑ hard shell

Ⓒ big horns

5. Look at the picture. Which tool mimics this bird's bill?

Ⓐ   Ⓑ   Ⓒ

6. Which body parts do animals use to take in oxygen? Choose all correct answers.

Ⓐ lungs

Ⓑ gills

Ⓒ fins

7. Engineers observed how bats use sound to find food. What tool did this help engineers invent?
   Ⓐ a fast train that is very quiet
   Ⓑ road markers that glow in the dark
   Ⓒ a machine that helps find fish

8. Why do trees grow new leaves in spring? Choose all correct answers.
   Ⓐ There is more sunlight.
   Ⓑ There is less sunlight.
   Ⓒ There is more water.

9. What body part helps this hawk find food?
   Ⓐ whiskers
   Ⓑ beak
   Ⓒ eyes

10. Why do gray whales swim to warmer waters in winter?
    Ⓐ to find fish to eat
    Ⓑ to have their young
    Ⓒ to escape danger

Unit 5
Living Things and Their Young

Unit Project • Compare Animals

How do wild animals and animals that live with people differ in how they care for their young? Investigate to find out.

Unit 5 At a Glance

Unit Vocabulary

parent a plant or animal that makes young like itself (p. 222)

offspring the young of a plant or animal (p. 222)

trait something that living things get from their parents (p. 231)

behavior a way an animal acts (p. 256)

Vocabulary Game • Guess the Word

Materials
- 1 set of word cards

How to Play
1. Work with a partner to make word cards.
2. Place the cards face down in a pile.
3. One player picks the top card but does not show it.
4. The second player asks questions until he or she guesses the word correctly.
5. Then the second player takes a card.

This field has plants that are of the same kind.

By the End of This Lesson
I will be able to explain how plants of the same kind can be alike and different.

Plants of the Same Kind

How are the young plants like the parent plant?
How are they different from the parent plant?

young plants

parent plant

Explore online.

Can You Explain It?

How can you tell if two plants
are the same kind of plant?

_____

_____

_____

Young and Old

Explore online.

young trees

parent trees

The young cherry trees do not have flowers yet. They will grow flowers.

A **parent** is a plant or animal that makes young similar to, but not exactly like, itself. Parent plants make young plants. The young plants may look different from the parent plants. But they will grow to look like the parent plants. **Offspring** are the young of a plant or an animal.

Circle the parts on the parent tree that are different from the parts on the young tree.

young tree   parent tree

Apply What You Know

Evidence Notebook • Do research. Draw pictures to show how a young plant may look different from its parent plant. Use evidence to tell how you know. Then look for patterns in your pictures.

Patterns
Go to the online handbook for tips.

Compare Parts

How are young plants and parent plants alike and different? Look closely at the pictures.

Explore online. ▶

young plant

parent plant

Most young plants have parts that look like the parts of their parents. The leaves may have the same shape. But the young plants may have smaller or fewer leaves.

✏️➡️ This leaf is from a parent tree. Circle the picture that shows its young.

Apply What You Know

Read, Write, Share! • Work in a small group. Choose an adult plant. Research what the plant looks like when it is young. Draw a picture to compare the young plant to the adult plant.

Participate in a Research Project
Go to the online handbook for tips.

Compare Adult Plants

How are adult plants of the same kind alike and different?

Explore online. ▶

These tulips are different heights.

The flowers of these tulips are different colors.

The leaves on these tulips have the same shape. But the leaves are not the same size.

✏️ This plant is a lily. Circle the picture that also shows a lily.

🖐 **Apply What You Know**

💡 **Patterns** Go to the online handbook for tips.

Evidence Notebook • Work in a group. Sort pictures of plants. Which are the same kind? Use patterns you observe to help you. Use evidence to explain how you sorted. Record in your Evidence Notebook.

Do the Math! • Work with a group. Find three plants. Use connecting cubes to find the height of each plant. Then compare the heights of your plants. Order them from shortest to tallest.

Compare and Order Length Go to the online handbook for tips.

Draw to show how you ordered. Write about what you did.

_____

_____

_____

_____

Name _____

Hands-On Activity
Grow Carrot Tops

Materials • two carrot tops • small bowl of water

Ask a Question

_____

Test and Record Data ▶ Explore online. ▶

Step 1

Place the bowl of carrots in a sunny place.

Step 2

Observe the carrots each day for ten days.
Record your observations.

Step 3

Compare the carrots. Look for patterns in their parts and size.

Step 4

Tell how plants of the same kind are the same and how they are different. Use the patterns you found as evidence.

_____

_____

_____

Make a claim that answers your question.

_____

_____

_____

What is your evidence?

_____

_____

_____

Take It Further

People in Science & Engineering •

Gregor Mendel

Explore more online.

Watch a Pumpkin Grow

Explore online. ▶

Gregor Mendel was a scientist. He used many pea plants to do experiments. He grew young plants from parent plants with different traits. A **trait** is something living things get from their parents.

Seed		Flower
Shape	Color	Color
Round	Yellow	White
Wrinkled	Green	Pink

Mendel looked at traits like seed shape, seed color, and flower color. He found that young plants had traits from both parents.

Mendel looked at how adult pea plants pass traits to their _____.

Ⓐ soil

Ⓑ roots

Ⓒ young

Lesson Check

young plants

Explore online. ▶

parent plant

Can You Explain It?

✏️ How can you tell if two plants are the same kind of plant? Be sure to

• Tell how plants of the same kind can be alike and different.

• Explain how you can observe patterns to tell if two plants are the same kind of plant.

_____

_____

_____

_____

(r) ©silkfactory/Getty Images

Self Check

1. How do most young plants and their parent plants look?

   Ⓐ exactly alike

   Ⓑ similar

   Ⓒ very different

2. Observe this young plant and its parent plant. What pattern do you see? Choose all correct answers.

   Ⓐ Their leaves are the same shape.

   Ⓑ Their leaves are purple and black.

   Ⓒ The young plant has more leaves than the parent plant.

young plant

parent plant

3. Cate sees a young plant in a park. She wants to find an adult plant that is the same kind of plant. What should Cate look for?

   Ⓐ a plant that is the same size

   Ⓑ a plant with the same number of leaves

   Ⓒ a plant with leaves that are like the young plant's leaves

4. Which plant is the parent of each young plant? Match the young to its parent.

5. Which statements are true?
Choose all correct answers.

Ⓐ All tulips are red.

Ⓑ Tulip flowers can be different colors.

Ⓒ Some tulips are taller than others.

How Do Animals Look Like Their Parents?

A young koala looks like its parent.

By the End of This Lesson
I will be able to tell how animals of the same kind can be alike and different.

Related Animals

Look at the adult swan and her young. What can you tell about the birds?

Explore online. ▶

Can You Solve It?

✏️ You see a young animal. You want to find an adult animal that is of the same kind. What should you look for?

_____

_____

_____

Animals Grow

Explore online. ▶

newborn

3 weeks old

3 months old

1 year old

   Parent animals make young animals like
themselves. Young animals are smaller
than their parents. They will grow to look
like their parents. Look at how a panda
changes as it grows into an adult.

adult

What is the same about a panda that is three months old and a panda that is an adult? Choose all correct answers.

Ⓐ They are the same size.

Ⓑ They have the same color fur.

Ⓒ They are the same shape.

✋ **Apply What You Know**

Evidence Notebook • Draw pictures to show an animal when it is young and when it is an adult. Talk with a partner about your animal. How does it grow and change? Use evidence to tell how you know. Look for patterns in your pictures.

💡 **Patterns** Go to the online handbook for tips.

Compare Parts

Explore online. ▶

An elephant parent has big ears and a long trunk. A young elephant has big ears and a long trunk, too.

A young rhino looks much like its parent, but it does not have a horn. It will grow a horn like its parent.

Think about young animals. How can you tell what kind of animal they are? One way is to look at their body parts. Most young animals have parts like their parents.

Hands-On Activity
Observe Brine Shrimp

Materials
- container with water
- brine shrimp eggs
- hand lens

Ask a Question

_____

Test and Record Data Explore online. ▶

Step 1

Add the brine shrimp eggs to the water.

Step 2

Observe the brine shrimp every other day for two weeks. Record your observations.

Lesson 2 • How Do Animals Look Like Their Parents?

Step 3

Compare the size, shape, and parts of the brine shrimp. How are the brine shrimp the same? How are they different? Use the patterns you found as evidence.

_____

_____

Make a claim that answers your question.

_____

_____

_____

What is your evidence?

_____

_____

_____

✏️ This is a young anteater. Circle the picture below that shows an adult anteater.

✋ **Apply What You Know**

Evidence Notebook • Observe animals. What body parts does each animal have? How can you tell if the animal is young or an adult? Use evidence to tell how you know. Record your answers.

💡 **Constructing Explanations and Designing Solutions**
Go to the online handbook for tips.

Compare Body Coverings

Some body coverings are scales, fur, or feathers. How are the body coverings of young animals and their parents alike and different?

Explore online. ▶

young raccoon

adult raccoon

Raccoons have dark fur around their eyes. The young and the adult have the same color fur.

young chicken

adult chicken

A young chick has yellow, fluffy feathers. It will grow new feathers and look more like its parent.

Observe each animal. Then draw a line to match each parent animal to its young.

Apply What You Know

Read, Write, Share! • Research an animal. Find out what its covering looks like when it is young and when it is an adult. Draw pictures to show what you found.

Participate in a Research Project Go to the online handbook for tips.

Animals of the Same Kind

How can animals of the same kind be alike and different?

Explore online. ▶

These fish are all the same kind. They have the same body parts. But they are not the same size. They also have different colors and markings.

These dogs are all the same kind. They all have four legs and a tail. They all have fur. But their fur is different colors.

Look at the animals. Circle the two that are the same kind of animal. Look for patterns.

Patterns Go to the online handbook for tips.

Do the Math! • Compare the dogs. Put them in order from shortest to tallest. Write 1, 2, or 3.

Compare and Order Length Go to the online handbook for tips.

_____ _____ _____

Apply What You Know

Evidence Notebook • Work with a partner. Look through books for animals of the same kind. Tell how they are alike and different. Use evidence to tell how you know. Draw the animals in your Evidence Notebook.

Take It Further
The Butterfly Life Cycle

Explore more online.

Pet Investigation

Explore online. ▶

Some young animals look very different from their parents. One example is a butterfly. A butterfly makes big changes as it grows. It begins its life inside an egg.

A caterpillar hatches from the egg.

The caterpillar becomes a pupa. It makes a hard covering.

An adult butterfly comes out of the covering. One day it may lay eggs.

Read, Write, Share!

✏️ What other questions do you have about the butterfly life cycle? Write your questions. Do research to answer them.

Ask and Answer Questions
Go to the online handbook for tips.

_____

_____

_____

✏️ Order the pictures to show the butterfly's life cycle. The first one is done for you.

1 _____

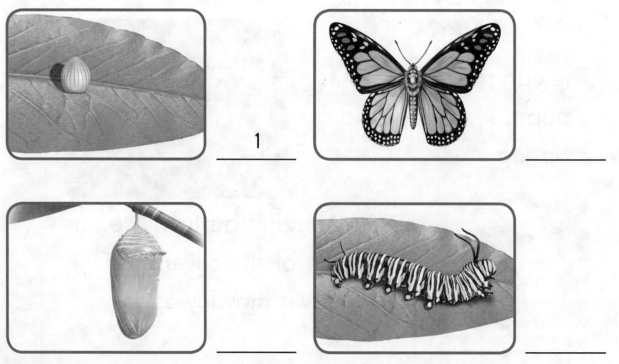

_____   _____

250

Lesson Check

Explore online. ▶

Can You Solve It?

✏️➤ You see a young animal. You want to find an adult animal that is the same kind. What should you look for? Be sure to

• Tell how animals of the same kind can be alike and different.

• Explain how you can observe patterns to tell if two animals are the same kind of animal.

_____

_____

_____

_____

Self Check

1. Which is true about most young animals and their parents? Choose all correct answers.

    Ⓐ Young animals have parts like their parents.

    Ⓑ Young animals grow to look like their parents.

    Ⓒ Young animals are bigger than their parents.

2. Marco sees a young animal that has scales on its body. What will the young animal's parent likely have?

    Ⓐ fur

    Ⓑ scales

    Ⓒ a shell

3. Observe each young animal and its parent. What pattern do you see?

    Ⓐ They are the same size.

    Ⓑ They have the same pattern on their fur.

    Ⓒ They have different body parts.

4. Which animal is the parent of each young?
   Match the parent to its young.

5. Amy observes two dogs that are the same kind.
   Which sentences could be true about the dogs?

   Ⓐ The dogs are different colors.

   Ⓑ One dog has fur and one dog has feathers.

   Ⓒ One dog is smaller than the other dog.

Animals care for their young in different ways.

By the End of This Lesson

I will be able to describe patterns in how animals help their young survive.

Animals Help Their Young

Explore online. ▶

Many animals help their young survive. This frog carries her tadpole up a tree. She puts it in water inside a flower. The tadpole gets what it needs to live and grow in the water.

Can You Explain It?

How do animals help their young survive?

By teaching them how to hunt.

Staying Safe

A **behavior** is a way an animal acts. What are some behaviors that help keep young animals safe?

Explore online. ▶

Young rabbits hide in grass while their mother is away. They wait for their mother to come back. They listen for her to call and then call back to her.

Prairie dogs live in groups. They bark to warn the group when danger is near.

Draw a line to match the animals to the words that tell how they stay safe.

hide to stay safe

bark when in danger

Do the Math! • One wolf spider carries 64 eggs in an egg sac. Another wolf spider carries 48 eggs. Which number of spider eggs is larger? Write <, >, or =.

Compare Numbers
Go to the online handbook for tips.

64  48

Apply What You Know

Evidence Notebook • Work with classmates. Find pictures of animals and their young staying safe. Talk about what the animals do to stay safe. Use evidence. Make a chart to show patterns.

Patterns • Obtaining, Evaluating, and Communicating Information
Go to the online handbook for tips.

Finding Food

Explore online.

Young robins make noise when they are hungry.

A mother sea lion calls to her pup to feed it. The pup calls back.

Animals need food to live. Many animals feed their young. Young animals show behaviors that help them get food from their parents.

✏️ **Circle the animal parent that feeds its young when the young make noise.**

✋ **Apply What You Know**

Evidence Notebook • Observe animals around your school. What are the animals doing to find food and survive? Use evidence to tell how you know. Talk with a partner. Make a chart to show the patterns you observe.

💡 **Patterns • Scientific Knowledge is Based on Empirical Evidence** Go to the online handbook for tips.

Young Animals Learn

Explore online.

Bear cubs learn to catch fish for food.

Leopard cubs learn to move around to stay safe.

Some young animals learn from their parents. They stay with their parents for a few years. They watch what their parents do to find food and stay safe.

What is this orangutan teaching its young to do?

Ⓐ find fruit

Ⓑ hide in a shelter

Ⓒ catch small animals

✋ **Apply What You Know**

Read, Write, Share! • Think about how different animal parents take care of their young. Work with a partner to answer these questions, How do the animals act the same? How do they act differently?

💡 **Recall Information • Ask and Answer Questions** Go to the online handbook for tips.

Hands-On Activity

Compare How Animals Learn

> **Materials** • a computer • animal books

Ask a Question

_____

Test and Record Data Explore online. ▶

Step 1

Work with a partner. Research polar bears and lions. Use a computer and animal books to collect information.

Step 2

Find out how polar bears and lions teach their young to find food. Find out how they teach their young to stay safe.

Step 3

Write or draw pictures to show what you found. Look for patterns in how the young animals learn from their parents.

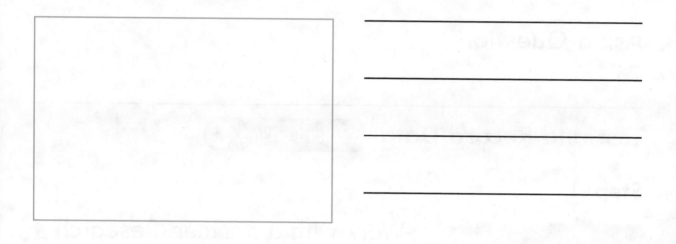

Make a claim that answers your question.

_____

_____

_____

What is your evidence?

_____

_____

_____

Take It Further
Careers in Science & Engineering •
Zookeeper

Explore more online.

On Their Own

Explore online. ▶

What does a zookeeper do? Zookeepers care for the animals in a zoo. They observe how animals act. They look for patterns to learn the best way to care for the animals.

Zookeepers give animals the food and water they need to live. They keep the animals and their environments clean.

✏️ Draw a line to match each picture to the words that tell about it.

| feeds animals | cleans environment | observes animals |

Do the Math! • Zoo A has 80 animals. Zoo B has 10 more animals than Zoo A. How many animals does Zoo B have?

Use Mental Math Go to the online handbook for tips.

Ⓐ 70

Ⓑ 81

Ⓒ 90

Lesson Check

Explore online. ▶

Can You Explain It?

✏️ How do animals help their young survive? Be sure to

- Describe patterns in how some animals act to take care of their young.
- Explain how this helps the young survive.

_____

_____

_____

_____

Self Check

1. How might an animal keep its young safe?
   Choose all correct answers.

   Ⓐ by feeding its young

   Ⓑ by calling to its young

   Ⓒ by hiding its young

2. Which animals stay safe in the same way?
   Match the animals.

3. Observe each bird and its young. What pattern do you see?

Ⓐ The parent bird is teaching its young to fly.

Ⓑ The parent bird is feeding its young.

Ⓒ The parent bird and its young are staying safe.

4. Which sentence is **true** about young animals?

Ⓐ Young animals make noise only when they are in danger.

Ⓑ All young animals make the same noises.

Ⓒ Some animals and their young make noises to find each other.

5. How long do bear cubs and leopard cubs stay with their mothers?

Ⓐ a few days

Ⓑ a few weeks

Ⓒ a few years

Unit 5 Performance Task

Match Animals and Their Young

Materials
- books about animals
- construction paper
- crayons
- scissors

STEPS

Step 1

Look in books to find out about animals and their young. Choose five kinds of animals.

Step 2

Cut ten cards from the paper. Make sure they are the same size.

Step 3

Draw adult animals on five of the cards. Draw their young on the other five cards.

© Houghton Mifflin Harcourt

Step 4

Put the cards face down on a table. Ask a friend to turn over two cards. If the cards match, tell how the adult and young are alike and different.

Step 5

Take turns flipping over the cards until all the adults and young are matched. What patterns do you see?

✔ Check

_____ I researched animals and their young.

_____ I made ten animal cards.

_____ I played a matching game.

_____ I compared animals and their young.

Name _____

1. Observe this young plant.
   Which plant is its parent?
   Look for patterns.

Ⓐ

Ⓑ

Ⓒ

2. How can plants of the same kind be different?
   Choose all correct answers.
   Ⓐ Their flowers can be different colors.
   Ⓑ They can have different numbers of leaves.
   Ⓒ They can grow different kinds of fruits.

3. Zak found a plant in his yard. He wants to find
   a young plant of the same kind. What should
   he look for?
   Ⓐ a smaller plant with bigger leaves
   Ⓑ a smaller plant with leaves that are the
      same shape
   Ⓒ a plant that is the same size

4. Which animal is the parent of each young? Match the young to its parent.

5. Kim sees an animal with fur on its body. What will a young animal of the same kind have on its body?
   Ⓐ feathers
   Ⓑ a shell
   Ⓒ fur

6. Which is true about young animals and their parents? Choose all correct answers.
   Ⓐ Young animals are smaller than their parents.
   Ⓑ Young animals are always different colors from their parents.
   Ⓒ Young animals are the same kind of animal as their parents.

7. Bella sees two horses that are the same kind, but they do not look exactly alike. How might they be different?
   Ⓐ They have different body coverings.
   Ⓑ They are different sizes.
   Ⓒ They have different numbers of legs.

8. Which are things an animal parent might teach its young? Choose all correct answers.
   Ⓐ how to stay safe
   Ⓑ how to find food
   Ⓒ how to make noise

9. Why do many young birds make noise?
   Ⓐ to find their way back home
   Ⓑ to hide from danger
   Ⓒ to help them get food from their parents

10. Which animals are feeding their young? Look for patterns. Choose all correct answers.

Unit 6

Objects and Patterns in the Sky

© Houghton Mifflin Harcourt

Unit Project • Explore the Moon's Phases

How can you model the moon's phases? Investigate to find out.

Unit 6 At a Glance

Unit Vocabulary

star an object in the sky that gives off its own light (p. 280)

sun the star closest to Earth (p. 280)

moon a large ball of rock that circles Earth (p. 286)

phases the moon's pattern of light and shadow as the moon moves (p. 288)

season a time of year with a certain kind of weather (p. 298)

Vocabulary Game • Show the Word

Materials
- 1 set of word cards

1. Work with a partner to make word cards.
2. Place the cards face down in a pile.
3. Pick a card, but do not show the word.
4. Draw or act out the word for your partner to guess.
5. When the word is guessed correctly, your partner picks a card to draw or act out.

Objects in the nighttime sky seem to change.

By the End of This Lesson
I will be able to describe objects in the sky and predict their patterns.

© Houghton Mifflin Harcourt • Image Credits: ©Abdul Aziz/Getty Images

Objects in the Sky

Explore online. ▶

daytime

nighttime

You can see objects in the daytime sky.

You can see objects in the nighttime sky.

Can You Explain It?

How do objects in the sky seem to change?

_____

_____

_____

_____

The Daytime Sky

Explore online.

sun from Earth

sun close up

You can see objects in the daytime sky. You may see the sun and sometimes the moon. The sun is a star. A **star** is an object in the sky. It gives off its own light. The **sun** is the star closest to Earth. It is made of hot gases. It gives off light and heat.

Underline two sentences that tell facts about the sun.

Apply What You Know

Evidence Notebook • Work with a partner. Talk about what you know about the sun in the daytime sky. Use evidence to tell how you know. Then write sentences about it in your Evidence Notebook.

Patterns in the Daytime Sky

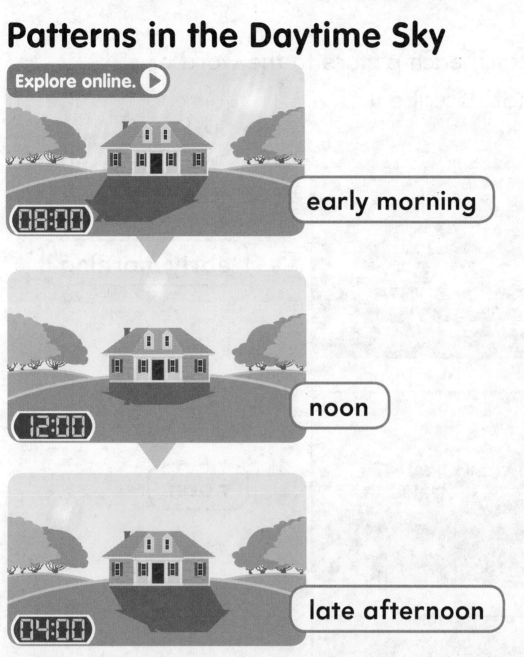

Explore online. ▶

early morning

08:00

noon

12:00

late afternoon

04:00

Each day, Earth turns all the way around. This makes the sun seem to move across the sky.

In early morning the sun seems low in the sky. At noon the sun seems to be directly above us. By late afternoon it seems to be low again, but on the other side of the sky. This pattern repeats each day.

Match each picture to the word or words that describe it.

early morning

noon

late afternoon

Name_____

Hands-On Activity
Observe the Pattern of the Sun

> Materials • drawing paper

Ask a Question

_____

Test and Record Data [Explore online. ▶]

Step 1

Choose a time in the morning. Record the time.

_____

Step 2

Go outside. Draw a picture to record the position of the sun. Be sure not to look directly at the sun.

Step 3

Look for an object that makes a shadow. Draw a picture of the object and its shadow.

Step 4

Repeat steps 2 and 3 at noon and again in the afternoon. Compare the position of the sun and the shadows at the different times of day.

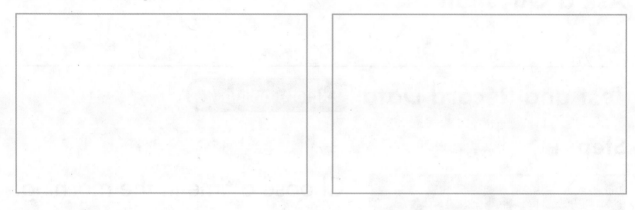

Step 5

Do the activity again another day.
What patterns do you see?

Make a claim that answers your question.

_____

_____

_____

What is your evidence?

_____

_____

Read, Write, Share! • Think about what you saw in the activity. Has the sun always seemed to move this way? Look in books or on the Internet to find out more.

Recall Information • **Order and Consistency** Go to the online handbook for tips.

✏️ Record what you think.

_____

_____

_____

_____

✋ **Apply What You Know**

Work with a partner. Make a model of the sun in the daytime sky. Use your model to explain the pattern of how the sun seems to move.

The Nighttime Sky

moon from Earth

Explore online.

moon close up

Night always follows day. On many nights you can see the moon in the sky. The **moon** is a large ball of rock that circles Earth. The moon seems to shine, but the moon does not give off its own light. The moon reflects light from the sun.

Write a fact about the moon.

_____

_____

_____

Explore online. ▶

On a clear night, you can see many stars. Stars are balls of hot gases. These gases give off light. This light is what you see from Earth. Stars look tiny because they are far away. A telescope can help you see them better. It makes objects look bigger.

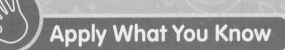 Underline the sentence that tells why you can see stars.

Apply What You Know

Work with a group. Make a picture dictionary about the nighttime sky. List the objects in the nighttime sky. Draw a picture for each object. Write sentences to tell about it.

Patterns in the Nighttime Sky

Explore online. ▶

new moon

first-quarter moon

full moon

third-quarter moon

The shape of the moon seems to change. These changes are called phases. **Phases** are the moon's pattern of light and shadow that you see as the moon moves. The phases repeat each month.

Patterns
Go to the online handbook for tips.

Do the Math! • ✏️⟹ Draw an X on the phase of the moon that looks like a whole circle. Draw a box around the phases that look like half of a circle.

Describe Shares Go to the online handbook for tips.

Explore online. ▶

These are stars you can see during the summer.

These are stars you can see during the winter.

The sun is the only star you can see during the day. But the stars you see each night are not always the same. They change with the seasons.

Which sentences are facts about the patterns of the stars? Choose all correct answers.

Ⓐ The sun is the only star you can see during the day.

Ⓑ The stars at night in the winter are the same as the stars at night in the summer.

Ⓒ You can see different stars at different times of the year.

Apply What You Know

Evidence Notebook • Work with a group. Make a model of the phases of the moon. Use your model to tell about the pattern of phases of the moon. How does the moon seem to change? Use evidence to tell how you know. Record your answers in your Evidence Notebook.

Take It Further

People in Science & Engineering •
Dr. Sarah Ballard

Explore more online.
Space Technology

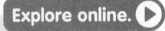

Explore online. ▶

Dr. Sarah Ballard is an astronomer.
An astronomer studies objects in the sky.
Dr. Ballard searches for new planets. A
planet is a large object in space that moves
around a sun or a star. Earth is a planet.

© Houghton Mifflin Harcourt

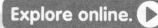

This is a model of a satellite that Dr. Ballard will use.

What do astronomers do? Choose all correct answers.

Ⓐ They study objects in the sky.

Ⓑ They find new planets.

Ⓒ They study animals.

Lesson Check

Name _____

daytime

Explore online. ▶

nighttime

Can You Explain It?

✏️➤ How do objects in the sky seem to change?

Be sure to

• Tell how objects seem to change in the sky.

• Describe the pattern of changes.

_____

_____

_____

_____

_____

Self Check

1. What causes the sun to seem to move in patterns?

   Ⓐ Earth turns all the way around.

   Ⓑ The sun turns all the way around.

   Ⓒ The moon turns all the way around.

2. Which words describe each picture? Write the words from the box to label each picture.

night	late afternoon	noon

   _____   _____   _____

3. How many times does the sun seem to rise in one week?

   Ⓐ 1

   Ⓑ 7

   Ⓒ 14

4. What is the moon?

Ⓐ a large star that circles Earth

Ⓑ a large ball of rock that circles Earth

Ⓒ a large ball of rock that blocks light from the sun

5. What are the phases of the moon? Write the numbers to show the correct order. The first one has been done for you.

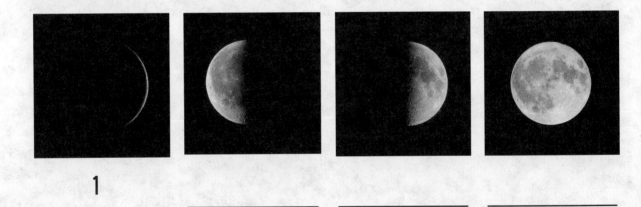

1 _____   _____   _____

6. What are the patterns of objects in the sky? Choose all correct answers.

Ⓐ The sun seems to move in the daytime sky.

Ⓑ All stars appear in the daytime sky.

Ⓒ The moon seems to change shape during the month.

What Are Patterns of Daylight?

Patterns of daylight change throughout the year.

By the End of This Lesson
I will be able to describe patterns of daylight.

Changing Seasons

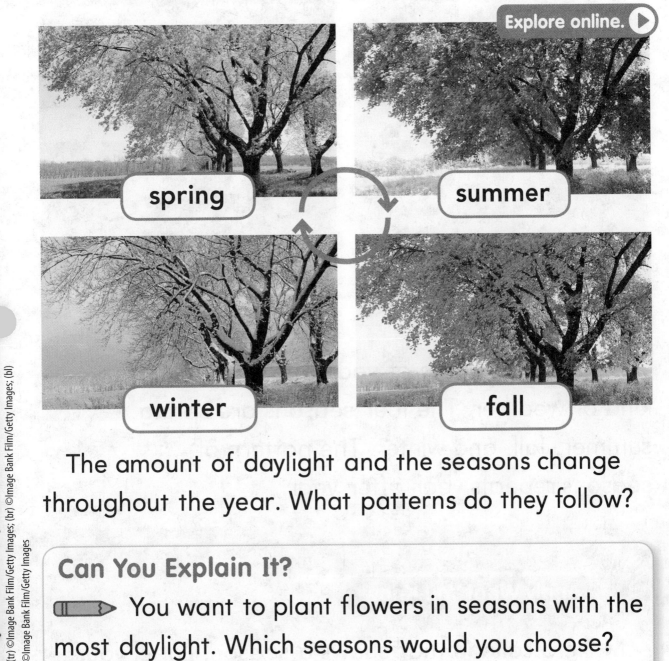

Explore online.

spring

summer

winter

fall

The amount of daylight and the seasons change throughout the year. What patterns do they follow?

Can You Explain It?

You want to plant flowers in seasons with the most daylight. Which seasons would you choose?

_____

_____

The Four Seasons

Explore online.

spring

summer

winter

fall

A **season** is a time of year with a certain kind of weather. The four seasons are spring, summer, fall, and winter. The pattern of seasons repeats year after year.

Apply What You Know

Make a collage that shows a season. Label your collage with the season. Write sentences to tell about it. Share your collage with the class.

Spring and Summer

Explore online.

Spring comes after winter. The air gets warmer. There are more hours of daylight than in winter. Spring days may be rainy, so people may wear light jackets. Warmer air and more daylight help plants begin to grow.

✏️ Write a sentence that describes spring.

_____

_____

_____

Explore online.

Summer follows spring. The first day of summer has the most hours of daylight. Summer days are often hot and sunny. People dress to stay cool. Flowers and fruit grow on plants.

Underline the sentence that describes summer weather.

Apply What You Know

Read, Write, Share! • Research spring and summer. Write two new facts about each season. Draw a picture for each fact. Then share your work. Compare facts. Did you find any patterns?

Patterns • Participate in a Research Project Go to the online handbook for tips.

Fall and Winter

Explore online.

    Fall comes after summer. There are fewer hours of daylight than in summer. Some animals store food for winter. The leaves of many trees change color and drop off. This is because there is less daylight.

✏️➡ Write a sentence that describes fall.

_____

_____

_____

Explore online.

Winter follows fall. The first day of winter has the fewest hours of daylight. Winter is the coldest time of year. Some places get snow. People wear coats to keep warm. Some animals grow thick fur.

✏️ Write a sentence that describes winter.

_____

_____

_____

Do the Math! • This chart shows the seasons that some children like best.

Solve Word Problems Go to the online handbook for tips.

Favorite Season	How Many?
Winter	II
Spring	TTHH
Summer	TTHH IIII
Fall	IIII

How many more children chose summer than spring?

Ⓐ 5   Ⓑ 3   Ⓒ 4

Apply What You Know

Read, Write, Share • **Evidence Notebook** • Why do you think the weather changes throughout the year? Use what you know about the seasons as evidence.

Recall Information Go to the online handbook for tips.

Patterns of Daylight

Explore online.

winter—4:43 at night

spring—7:13 at night

summer—8:29 at night

fall—6:57 at night

The amount of daylight changes from season to season. The sun rises and sets at different times during the year. This pattern repeats each year. Take a look at what time the sun sets in one place at the start of each season.

Apply What You Know

Evidence Notebook • Work with a partner. Use evidence to explain the patterns of daylight during the year. Write your explanations in your Evidence Notebook.

Hands-On Activity

Observe Patterns of Sunset

Materials	• a calendar	• a computer
	• crayons	• drawing paper

Ask a Question

_____

Test and Record Data Explore online. ▶

Step 1

Identify the season and the date. Together, look up what time the sun will seem to set that day.

Step 2

Look up what time the sun will seem to set on a day in the next two seasons.

Step 3

Compare all the times you found. Record any patterns.

Make a claim that answers your question.

_____

_____

_____

_____

_____

What is your evidence?

_____

_____

_____

_____

Take It Further

Careers in Science & Engineering •
Circadian Biologist

Explore more online.
The Midnight Sun

Explore online. ▶

Circadian biologists study how seasons and daylight affect living things.

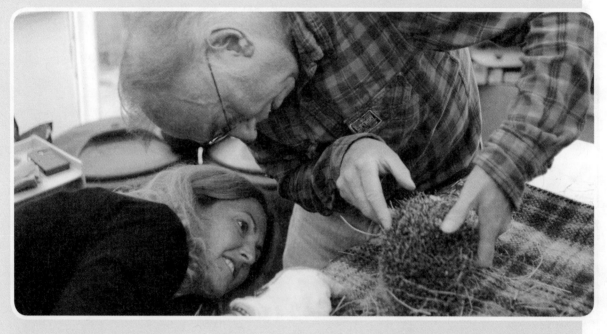

You may feel sleepier in fall and winter. Circadian biologists found out why. There is less daylight in fall and winter. This makes you feel sleepier.

Less daylight affects animals, too. They sense that it is time to get ready for winter.

Think about the people and animals in your home or community. How do the seasons affect them? How do they change?

> ✏️ Draw a picture to show what happens. Then write about it.

_____

_____

_____

Lesson Check

spring

summer

winter

fall

Explore online. ▶

Can You Explain It?

✏️ You want to plant flowers in seasons with the most daylight. Which seasons would you choose?

Be sure to

• Tell how knowing patterns of daylight helped you solve the problem.

_____

_____

_____

Self Check

1. Write the numbers 2, 3, and 4 to show the order of the seasons. The first one has been done for you.

spring	winter	fall	summer
1	_____	_____	_____

2. This family is eating dinner at the same time in winter and summer. Which is true about when the sun seems to set?

winter   summer

Ⓐ The sun seems to set earlier in summer.

Ⓑ The sun seems to set earlier in winter.

Ⓒ The sun seems to set at the same time in winter and summer.

3. Spring and fall have about the same number of hours of _____.

Ⓐ rain

Ⓑ sunset

Ⓒ daylight

4. If the sun seems to set at 7 o'clock on the first day of spring, when will it seem to set on the first day of summer?

Ⓐ earlier than 7 o'clock

Ⓑ later than 7 o'clock

Ⓒ at the same time

5. Which is a pattern of daylight?

Ⓐ The amount of daylight changes from day to day with the seasons.

Ⓑ The amount of daylight changes from year to year.

Ⓒ The amount of daylight never changes.

Unit 6 Performance Task
Explore Short and Long Days

Materials
- two seedlings of the same kind
- water
- paper clips

STEPS

Step 1

Label one seedling **winter** and the other seedling **spring**. Measure the height of each seedling with paper clips. Record your observations.

Step 2

Place the seedlings in a sunny window. After one hour, put the **winter** seedling in a dark place. Leave the **spring** seedling in the sunny window.

Step 3

Put the **winter** seedling in the window for only one hour each day.

Step 4

Observe the seedlings for two weeks. Water the soil when it is dry. Measure and record the results every day.

Step 5

Use evidence to tell why a plant in spring might grow more than a plant in winter. Compare your results with the results of other classmates.

✔ Check

_____ I gave the **spring** seedling long days of sunlight.

_____ I gave the **winter** seedling short days of sunlight.

_____ I observed the seedlings for two weeks and recorded my observations every day.

_____ I explained why a plant in spring might grow more than a plant in winter.

_____ I compared my results to the results of my classmates.

Name _____

1. Which objects give off their own light?
   Choose all correct answers.
   Ⓐ moon
   Ⓑ sun
   Ⓒ star

2. When does the sun seem to rise?
   Ⓐ in the morning
   Ⓑ at noon
   Ⓒ at night

3. Look at the shadow in the picture.
   Where does the sun seem to be?
   Ⓐ low in the morning sky
   Ⓑ high in the noon sky
   Ⓒ low in the afternoon sky

4. Which pattern repeats every day?
   Ⓐ The sun seems to move across the sky.
   Ⓑ The shape of the moon seems to change.
   Ⓒ The seasons change.

5. What phase of the moon does the picture show?

Ⓐ new moon

Ⓑ half moon

Ⓒ full moon

6. Look at the pictures. Which word describes each picture? Write a word from the word box.

| fall | spring | summer | winter |

_____ _____ _____ _____

7. Which season follows summer?

Ⓐ spring

Ⓑ fall

Ⓒ winter

8. Which statements are true about fall?
   Choose all correct answers.
   Ⓐ There are fewer hours of daylight than summer.
   Ⓑ Some animals move to warmer places.
   Ⓒ People dress to stay cool.

9. Which day of the year has the most hours
   of daylight?
   Ⓐ the first day of winter
   Ⓑ the first day of spring
   Ⓒ the first day of summer

10. How is winter different from summer?
    Ⓐ Winter has fewer hours of daylight than
       summer.
    Ⓑ Winter has more hours of daylight than
       summer.
    Ⓒ Winter has the same number of hours of
       daylight as summer.

Interactive Glossary

This Interactive Glossary will help you learn how to spell and define a vocabulary term. The Glossary will give you the meaning of the term. It will also show you a picture to help you understand what the term means.

Where you see , write your own words or draw your own picture to help you remember what the term means.

adaptation

Something that helps a living thing survive in its environment. (p. 198)

behavior

A way an animal acts. (p. 256)

Interactive Glossary

communicate

To share information. (p. 60)

design process

A plan with steps that help engineers find good solutions. (p. 20)

engineer

A person who uses math and science to solve problems. (p. 6)

environment

All the living and nonliving things in a place. (p. 198)

gills

Body parts that take in oxygen from water. (p. 183)

light

Energy that lets you see. (p. 84)

Interactive Glossary

lungs

Body parts that take in air. (p. 183)

mimic

To copy. (p. 147)

moon

A large ball of rock that circles Earth. (p. 286)

© Houghton Mifflin Harcourt • Image Credits: (t) ©Sergio Pitamitz/National Geographic/Getty Images; (c) ©Lex Aalders/EyeEm/Getty Images; (b) ©Avalon

offspring

The young of a plant or animal. (p. 222)

parent

A plant or animal that makes young like itself. (p. 222)

phases

The moon's pattern of light and shadow that you see as the moon moves. (p. 288)

Interactive Glossary

pitch

How high or low a sound is. (p. 47)

problem

Something that needs to be fixed or made better. (p. 6)

reflect

To bounce back from a surface. (p. 118)

season

A time of year with a certain kind of weather. (p. 298)

shadow

A dark spot made when an object blocks light. (p. 104)

solution

Something that fixes a problem. (p. 6)

Interactive Glossary

sound

A kind of energy you hear when something vibrates. (p. 44)

star

An object in the sky that gives off its own light. (p. 280)

sun

The star closest to Earth. (p. 280)

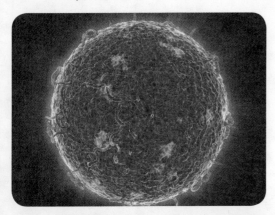

technology

What engineers make to meet needs and solve problems. (p. 9)

trait

Something living things get from their parents. (p. 231)

vibrate

To move quickly back and forth. (p. 44)

Interactive Glossary

volume

How loud or soft a sound is.
(p. 46)

Index

Index

Index

Index

noon, daytime sky at, 281, 282

nose, animal
  to find food, 179, 202
  to notice things, 202

**notes, communicating
  solutions with,** 25

O

objects. *See also* **sky,
  objects in the**
  light hitting, 115
  light passing
  through, 100–103
  movement of, 43
  observed in different
  amounts of light,
  87–88
  packaging, 14
  seen in different
  amounts of light,
  87–89
  seen in the dark,
  84–85, 86, 89–92
  sound causing
  movement of, 50–52
  that are technology, 9
  that make sound,
  63–65

observations
  brine shrimp,
  241–242
  by zookeepers, 265
  engineers making, 7

made in different
amounts of light,
87–88
of pattern of the
sun, 283–284
of patterns of
daylight, 305–306
plant growth,
199–200

ocean sponge, 191

offspring, 222. *See
  also* **young animals;
  young plants**

orangutan, 262

P

packaging engineer,
  13–14

panda, 238–239

paper airplane, 168

parent, 222

parent animals
  feeding their young,
  259–260
  helping their young,
  255–257
  young animals
  having body parts
  like, 240
  young animals
  learning from,
  261–262
  young animals
  looking different
  from, 237

young animals
looking like, 238–239

parent plants. *See*
  adult plants

parent tree, 222, 223

patterns
  in the daytime sky,
  281–285
  in the nighttime sky,
  288–290
  observing daylight,
  305–306
  of daylight through
  the year, 297–304
  of the sun, 283–284

penguins, 205

**People in Science &
  Engineering**
  Ballard, Sarah,
  291–292
  Beethoven, Ludwig
  van, 53–54
  Benyus, Janine,
  153–154
  Delaney, Mary, 29
  Edison, Thomas,
  93–94
  Mendel, Gregor,
  231–232

phases of the moon,
  288

phones, 67

**photos,
  communicating
  solution with,** 25

piano, pitch on, 47

Index

Index